THE RESTORATION, 1660–1688

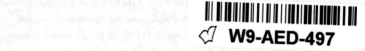

British History in Perspective
General Editor: Jeremy Black

THE RESTORATION

PAUL SEAWARD

MACMILLAN

First published 1991

Published by
MACMILLAN EDUCATION LTD
Houndmills, Basingstoke, Hampshire RG21 2XS
and London
Companies and representatives
throughout the world

Typeset by LBJ Enterprises Ltd
Chilcompton and Tadley

Printed in Hong Kong

British Library Cataloguing in Publication Data
Seaward, Paul
The Restoration, 1660–1688. — (British history in
perspective, ISSN 0955–8322)
1. England, 1660–1688
I. Title   II. Series
942.066
ISBN 0–333–48052–X
ISBN 0–333–48053–8 pbk

Contents

Preface

The following study is intended as a brief introduction to some of the themes of Restoration politics. The limitations of my knowledge and its space prevent it from being in any way comprehensive. I have tried principally to give some sense of the character of politics, the things that worried politicians, and to discuss the sources of instability in post-revolution England. I hope that the bibliography indicates where greater enlightenment on issues that I have dealt with cursorily or not at all may be found. I am grateful to Dr C.G.A. Clay and Cambridge University Press, for permission to reproduce the table on p. 74; to John Morrill, Jonathan Scott, John Spurr and Colin Lee for reading and commenting on the text, and for all of their suggestions; to Vanessa Graham, of Macmillan, for her forbearance; and to Hilary, for her patience and much else.

P.S.

1

INTRODUCTION

The death of Oliver Cromwell, in September 1658, put an end to the delicate balance of legitimacy and naked force which his rule had represented. In the following twenty months, the complicated constitutions, the military might, the carefully flaunted moderation by which both Commonwealth and Protectorate had sought to preserve their power, all disintegrated. By the winter of 1659, the restoration to power of the Rump Parliament indicated the exhaustion of the constitutional imagination. Whatever he intended – whether to seize power himself, or to engineer a royal restoration – the intervention of General Monck, the conservative commander of the army in Scotland, sealed the fate of England's republican experiment. In the early months of 1660 Monck forced the Rump to accede to popular pressure and readmit those of its members who had been excluded in 1648; the reunited body's decision to dissolve itself and call new elections was then inevitable. Despite the formal exclusion of royalists from candidacy, the new parliament, or Convention, was royalist enough when it assembled on 25 April to begin negotiations with Charles II, in exile across the Channel in the Netherlands. On 29 April it voted to restore him, and a month later he entered London for the first time since 1642, as its people went jubilant with relief.

For the England to which the monarchy was restored seemed to be suffused with royalist sentiment. The king, wrote

1

the London barber Thomas Rugg, was 'by a general vogue' invited back; 'the people', reminisced the lord chancellor, the Earl of Clarendon, were 'admirably disposed and prepared to pay all the subjection, duty and obedience, that a just and prudent king could expect from them'.[1] Yet Clarendon was deeply aware that the Restoration was only the beginning of a long process of political recovery. Its central questions were to preoccupy him and his successors for years to come: what were the lasting effects on the position of the monarchy and the Church of parliamentary power, the execution of the king, religious toleration? Was there any prospect of restoring the unity of a nation so divided by the partisan hatreds and private interests that had been thrown up by twenty years of disputed rule? Was it possible to recreate peace and prosperity in what was still, for all the rejoicing at the Restoration, a bitterly divided and politically unconfident country?

Restoration England was a state on probation. To a country which had been accustomed to thinking of itself as God's chosen nation, a modern protestant Israel, the dismal history of the past twenty years had seemed to be evidence of the withdrawal of his favour. For a considerable majority, the Restoration appeared to show that he had relented: but it was clear that Englishmen could no longer take their deliverance for granted. Her neighbours were equally sceptical of the permanence of England's restored stability: it was a country which had in the last half-century changed from one of the more peaceful and successful of monarchies to the sick man of Europe, a country which, as the French bishop and theologian Bossuet said in his sermon at the funeral of Charles I's queen, had been plagued by a disrespect for authority and a continual itch for change.[2] In their mood of pessimistic conservatism, many English writers agreed. Thomas Otway's play of 1681, *Venice Preserv'd*, conveyed a common belief in England's turbulence: 'You are an Englishman' one of its characters was told: 'when treason's hatching/ One might have thought you'd not have been far behind hand'.[3] A passion for change, a hatred for stability, seemed to be the country's vice and its downfall. The sense of impermanence, and the desire for permanence, pervaded English politics.

The immanence of political violence added to the feeling of uncertainty. Throughout the 1660s, 1670s and 1680s the country was periodically terrorised by rumours of conspiracy, invasion, assassination and rebellion. Little violence actually occurred – a small, if terrifying, rising of religious radicals convulsed London for almost a week in January 1661, and there were real, if ineffective, rebellions in Yorkshire and in Ireland in 1663 – but throughout the period networks of dedicated opponents of the regime, republicans and religious radicals, were working in one way or another for its destruction. Underlying Restoration politics was the fear that these subterranean rumblings might erupt with volcanic violence, blowing apart the weak crust of society and hierarchy. If government was shaken, Sir John Holland told parliament in the early 1660s, 'we must unavoidably fall into the hands of unreasonable men, into the hands of an insolent, violent, merciless, frantic, fanatic generation of people, who in hatred to monarchy, magistracy and ministry, would soon destroy all the nobility, gentry, persons of interest and quality throughout the nation'.[4] The shadow of 1641 fell across every crisis, major or minor; the reaction to political events, even in the volume of land sales, indicated a keen anxiety about political stability.[5] Each new *frisson* emphasised that what England needed, above all, was peace and stability, a reassurance against the tyranny and oppression of the Protectorate and the chaos and anarchy of the years since its demise.

The threat of violence seemed only a symptom, however, of the central uncertainty of Restoration politics. The heretical view that England's ancient constitution was itself the cause of instability was horribly shocking to those who had been brought up to regard it as the very perfection of political systems. But James Harrington was by no means the only person to argue (as he did in his *Oceana* of 1656) that the distribution of political power – principally in the hands of the king and nobility – no longer reflected the balance of economic strength and that sooner or later the disjunction would have to be reflected in a change of political structure.[6] Thomas Hobbes, too, in his *Leviathan* of 1651, cast doubt on the constitution's viability because a system in which legislative power was divided from executive power, and in which the law was claimed to be superior to the sovereign power, was bound to end in competition for political dominance: what was needed was a sovereign with incontrovertible, undivided authority.[7] A country celebrated for its successful (though the success was much overblown) compromise between popular and autocratic rule found itself struggling to retain the balance between liberty and authority; a country which had come to view political change as more likely to destroy political stability than to restore it, dismissed Harrington as republican and Hobbes as godless. All the same, it put its politicians on their guard for signs that the arguments of either had found greater resonance with the government itself.

If political change did not finally kill off the old order, social and economic change might. Harrington had claimed the gentry as the newly wealthy of seventeenth-century England; the gentry themselves were not so certain. For a century and a half, the prices of agricultural commodities had been buoyed up by a rapidly growing population and a general inflation. Land rents and values had risen accordingly, and the gentry, living mainly from renting out farming land, had profited greatly. But in the mid-seventeenth century population growth slackened and virtually stopped. Farmers found that instead of constantly striving to keep up with demand, they were now overproducing. Prices, particularly of grain, dropped heavily. Between 1640 and 1750 prices of agricultural products rose by no more than 2 per cent. Farmers who failed to diversify could barely cover their costs: as Lord North remarked in 1669, 'never was there more need of good managery than now, at a time when revenues of the gentry are fallen beyond what could have been imagined of late years'.[8]

The decline in their rental revenue threatened not only the country gentry's income, but also their social standing. Sir Henry Lee's rents were in 1666 'so ill paid that he gives over house and goes to sojourn with a friend in Wiltshire . . . many more . . . are now breaking up house and coming to London to save charges for they cannot get rents to defray the expenses of a numerous family of servants'.[9] Gentlemen who were unable to dominate their localities by their presence, unable to maintain their contacts with the other gentry of the area, who no longer sat regularly on the magistrates' bench, who failed to impress their neighbours by the lavishness of their entertainment, would lose a good deal of their social and political power. Others seemed ready to take it up. The Civil War had brought into politics and administration people who had before been seen merely as the recipients of government, not its dispensers. 'Our posterity will say that to deliver them from the yoke of the king we have subjected them to that of the common people', thundered the Earl of Essex in the 1640s; 'I thought it a crime to be a nobleman', wrote the parliamentarian Lord Willoughby of Parham.[10] A horrified gentry complained that artisans – tinkers, pedlars, cobblers – who had set themselves up in county committees during the Interregnum were usurping the deference and power which was their due. Gentry anxiously watched the assertiveness of their social inferiors as the decline in population growth led to constriction in the labour market. Employers tried vainly to hold down wages and force labourers and servants to work.[11] Royalist gentry, banned for so long from participation in government and weakened by the discriminatory taxes and penalties which had been laid on them during the Civil War and Interregnum, were already unsure whether they would be able to re-establish their social dominance. They, in particular, bitterly resented what they saw as the rise of a 'new gentry' of merchants, their wealth based on trade, on financial dealing with the revolutionary regimes and often, they thought (through dealing in mortgages, buying and selling royalists' lands), on their own sufferings. The poet Alexander Brome satirised these social climbers, who

> In pomp, attire, and every thing they did
> Look like true *Gentry*, but the *soul* and *head*
> . . . What *Nobility*
> Sprung in an instant from all trade had we.[12]

Such men, complained the moralist and scholar Edward Waterhouse in 1665, had by corruption 'established themselves in prosperity (while others that lost estates . . . are in a great measure impoverished and by reason thereof obscured)'.[13] Even if they ignored Harrington's complex arguments, the gentry were well aware of their central premiss: that political influence rested with these who held economic power. In the longer term, into the eighteenth century, the greater gentry at least would consolidate their wealth and confirm their social influence and political power. But for now, there was no way of telling what the future might hold. Would Civil War and agricultural recession mean a decline in their relative wealth? And would that mean the erosion of their traditional alliance with the crown to rule the country?

The Church had always been a third party to that alliance, its parish priests providing the moral foundations of the government's power. But the future of the Church was itself uncertain. Even if it managed to regain the monopolistic position it had held in the religious life of pre-Civil War England, would it be able to regain the hearts and minds of the many people who had shown little love for its hierarchy, and who had been tempted in their thousands into the numerous sects that had sprung up during the Civil War, or who sought in presbyterianism a more reformed protestant church than the Church of England? It was a question of more than purely religious significance to a country which saw disunity in religion as bound to provoke political disorder. 'When people separate and rendezvous themselves into distinct sects and parties', wrote Samuel Parker, one of the Church's foremost (if least subtle) controversialists, they become 'destructive of the common peace and amity of mankind';[14] the young John Locke, writing in 1661, agreed that those who held differing religious opinions were dangerous to themselves and to society: 'the overheated zeal of these who know how to arm the rash folly of the ignorant and passionate multitude with the authority of conscience often kindles a blaze among the populace capable of consuming everything'.[15]

Political, economic, religious change, all threatened the country with violence and the gentry with the loss of their power. There was no need for it, conservatives endlessly argued: change came not from necessity, but from those who wanted change for change's sake, or who plotted out of personal ambition. Royalist accounts of the Civil War put its origins down to a conspiracy of puritans, eager for power beyond their station; even parliamentarian historians rarely claimed that the war's origins lay in the failure of a system, rather than in the abuse of it.[16] Even if the need for change was acknowledged, it was normally insisted that it needed to be by evolution, not revolution. The use of politics to amend the diseases of the state was condemned as a difficult art; that it would work, a dangerous delusion. The attempt to bring down arbitrary rule in 1640 had ended in anarchy and Civil War, and ultimately Cromwellian tyranny. 'By innovations, especially sudden [ones]', wrote one of the many who argued the dangers of precipitate change, 'the minds of men are disquieted, fuel is brought into fiery and turbulent spirits, and the peace of the Church and Commonwealth endangered, if not destroyed.'[17]

The country was too preoccupied with its own problems in 1660 to look very far beyond its coasts. But the future of England's foreign relations was almost as uncertain and as complex a question for the new government as were the future constitution of Church and State. The exploits at sea and abroad of the republic's and Cromwell's navy and army had given Englishmen a new sense of international power and confidence, even as they had felt a decline of constitutional confidence at home; in time, too, the country at large would become deeply concerned with the politics of continental Europe as they came to seem closely intertwined with its own. For the moment, however, Englishmen were anxiously wondering whether or not the replacement of a 'mountebank' by a 'lawfull' government, as Sir Justinian Isham put it, would provide them with the stability they craved.[18] 'There was in no conjuncture more need', wrote Clarendon of the Restoration, that the virtue and wisdom and industry of a prince should be evident, and made manifest in the preservation of his dignity, and in the application of his mind to the government of his affairs; and that all who were eminently trusted by him should be men of unquestionable sincerity, who with industry and dexterity should first endeavour to compose the public disorders, and to provide for peace and settlement of the kingdom, before they applied themselves to make or improve their own peculiar fortunes.[19]

To most of the country Charles II and his younger brother were strangers. The king had been abroad since 1646, when he was sixteen, apart from his brief and ignominious attempt in 1651 to regain his throne by invasion from Scotland. James, the Duke of York, had escaped from parliamentary custody in 1648: he had never returned, until now, to England. The royalist press reported Charles (fairly) to be charming, affable and intelligent: his lack of interest in the details of government, his deep political cynicism, his indecisiveness were ignored. The English public knew, a little, of James's distinguished military career with the French and Spanish armies: they were to find out about his loyalty and determination, but also about his authoritarianism. If James often made his attitude to politics perfectly plain, the king's own mind was opaque, and his policies mysterious.

Neither king, by consistently employing ministers and advisers from a single political tradition, firmly identified himself with any one approach to the political problems which beset the nation. Anglican royalists had established the clearest title to the confidence of the king: throughout the Civil War and Interregnum they had combined unceasing loyalty to the monarchy with dedication to the cause of the Church of England. Many of them had joined with Charles in exile: the Earl of Clarendon, his lord chancellor; the Duke of Ormonde, the lord lieutenant of Ireland; Sir Edward Nicholas, one of his secretaries of state until 1662; Henry Coventry, another secretary of state, from 1672 to 1680. Some who maintained their loyalty and patronage of the Church while remaining at home also became ministers: the Earl of Southampton, the lord treasurer until 1667, was the most celebrated and respected. There were those of the same stamp, too young to participate in the Civil War themselves, who came to prominence after the Restoration: Sir Heneage Finch, solicitor-general, and eventually Earl of Nottingham and lord chancellor; and Clarendon's sons, the Hyde brothers, eventually the second Earl of Clarendon and the Earl of Rochester.

Even among these, however, there were nuances of opinion: lawyers such as Clarendon possessed a profound respect for the English constitution and the law which not all royalists shared. Both Clarendon and Southampton had themselves been involved in the demand for reform of government abuses in 1640 and 1641, before joining Charles I's services. And not all royalists had the commitment to the Church that these had; the Earl of Bristol, also an exile and a favourite and adviser of Charles II, though never his minister, had converted to Roman Catholicism during the Interregnum. Sir Henry Bennet, later Earl of Arlington, and secretary of state from 1662 to 1674, was likewise in exile with the court in the 1650s; though he was originally intended for the Church, he seemed to have little affection for it, and on his deathbed was converted to Roman Catholicism. The Duke of Buckingham, who achieved a central place in the king's counsels in the late 1660s and early 1670s, had been in exile, and had fought for the king; but no one seemed to think him of any religion at all, and his contacts with the radical sects seemed to place him well beyond the anglican royalist pale.

'Presbyterians', by which were usually meant those former puritans who had espoused parliament's cause in the 1640s while rejecting the execution of Charles I and the regimes which followed it, were also brought in to the king's counsels, to the disgust of many royalists. They, after all, in the shape of General Monck, the excluded members of the Long Parliament, and the Convention, had been principally responsible for the king's Restoration. Monck himself was created Duke of Albemarle and made commander of the army; Edward Montague, Cromwell's commander of the navy, was translated to the same position under the monarchy. Various other presbyterian leaders – the Earl of Manchester, Lord

Robartes, Sir Harbottle Grimston – received important posts in the royal household or in the law; and the Earl of Lauderdale came (though by abandoning his commitment to presbyterianism) to exercise a dominant position in Scotland until 1680. There were also those able young administrators and politicians who had made a name for themselves under Cromwell: a few men such as Anthony Ashley Cooper, who became chancellor of the exchequer and eventually lord chancellor and Earl of Shaftesbury, managed to secure places of power under Charles II, despite opinions on the religious question which horrified many of their colleagues.

Throughout 1660, the final intentions of Charles and his ministers remained obscure. For the rest of the year, the Convention continued to sit, sorting out some of the immediate problems of the new regime. The government avoided (its first hurdle) the imposition of any conditions on its restoration or constitutional limits to its power beyond those which Charles I and his predecessors had assented to; the court secured the Convention's co-operation in the disbandment of the army; it obtained a settlement of royal finances which, in theory at least, guaranteed a stable income to meet the ordinary expenses of government; and it offered a liberal temporary settlement of the religious problem, while avoiding any permanent, far-reaching change in the Church. By December 1660, when the Convention Parliament was dissolved, legally – if not quite in practice – the country had almost the same form of government as it had had shortly before the outbreak of war, after the earliest reforms of the Long Parliament. Whether the king regarded the powers it gave him as sufficient, whether they could preserve the monarchy against future storms, whether he could, or would, defend the Church against the pressure of differing sects and opinions, remained to be seen.

2

CONFLICTS OF POWER

Uncertain of the limits and durability of their real power, both government and the social elite would try, in the ensuing years, to ensure its permanence and re-establish its boundaries. Yet the power of the two was not always complementary. The elite thought it was: England's traditions of self-government meant that ruling was largely a matter of close co-operation between central government and the local aristocracy and gentry, both in making laws in parliament and in executing them in the country. Almost every law, every convention, was underpinned by the notion that English government was in practice a collaborative affair. For the Crown, however, those traditions, laws and conventions might be seen as part of the problem. It was, after all, possible to take the view that England's system of self-government was largely responsible for the collapse of royal power in the 1640s – as, indeed, had Thomas Hobbes. The Earl of Peterborough made the absolutist's point early on after the Restoration: 'these old notions, of mixed governments, privileges and conditions have by several accidents of state been put out of the essence of things, and they are not to be practised any longer'.[1]

Parliament embodied the collaborative traditions of English government; but Civil War had naturally enhanced the court's suspicion of it. The rebellion of the Long Parliament had shown how easily it could become a vehicle for consolidating opposition to the government, be manipulated by factions attempting to gain power and influence with the king, or even expand its own role and function at the expense of royal authority. Even the Earl of Clarendon, one of the most phlegmatic of Charles II's ministers and a man dedicated to the preservation of the constitution, complained of the 'usurpations in both houses of parliament since the year 1640', and 'many other excesses, which had been affected by both before that time under the name of privileges', as well as the tendency of the House of Commons to encroach upon the powers of the Lords.[2] Many other ministers were disturbed and shocked by the periodic turbulence of parliaments: 'I cannot but observe to your grace by what we see here', wrote the secretary of state to the lord lieutenant of Ireland in 1663, 'that the king's power is not so easily restored by parliament as it is retrenched'.[3] In 1679 the Earl of Danby, a former lord treasurer, believed that parliament was aiming to take complete control of the government.[4]

Historians used to agree with them. The fact that the Revolution of 1689 and its aftermath resulted in a permanent expansion of parliamentary power made it tempting to believe that parliament's pre-eminence in the 1640s was a sign of a political development that would be irresistible in the long run, and which the restoration of the old norms of political life might delay, but never prevent. Historians claimed that parliament's exercise of real power during the 1640s had raised its prestige and its members' ambitions, so that it could never again be looked upon as a subordinate part of government: even the loyal parliaments of the Restoration shared their predecessors' assertiveness. The affirmation of both Houses of 1 May 1660 that 'according to the ancient and fundamental laws of this kingdom, the government is and ought to be, by King, Lords and Commons' (where previously the legislative power had been described as the 'King in parliament') seemed to claim for parliament a position no longer inferior, but equal, or 'co-ordinate' with the king.[5]

Few would now accept this image of a parliament deliberately seeking to enlarge its own field of competence. It would have been difficult to find a member of the Restoration House of Commons or House of Lords who wished to see parliament with real executive power; still more one who seriously maintained that the Commons and the Lords were equal partners with the king in a governmental trinity.[6] The proper relationship of Crown and parliament they regarded to be one of mutual respect and co-operation, not of competition for power; when they argued over constitutional issues, the arguments had normally originated in more short-term political disagreements, not in portentous struggles for power between rival institutions. A few republicans looked back on the achievements and prestige of parliaments in the 1640s and 1650s with pride; but many more partisans on all sides found as much to deplore as to admire. Royalists regarded the Long Parliament as having been corrupted by a minority of religious zealots; anglicans and presbyterians alike held the Rump's regicide in religious horror; Barebone's and the Protectorate parliaments had been notable for little but partisan squabbles and political impotence. The Convention of 1660 may have done something to restore parliament's reputation by restoring the king and the old order; but its successor, the Cavalier Parliament, quickly forfeited popular respect as it gained a reputation for corruption that almost paralleled that of the Long Parliament. Even those members of Restoration parliaments who had also served in the Long Parliament, the Rump or Protectorate parliaments, tended to see them as examples to be avoided, rather than followed. It was easy to be cynical and sceptical about parliaments and the politicians that filled them: 'the members of the House of Commons', wrote the satirist Samuel Butler a few years after the Restoration, 'are but a kind of botchers and [menders] of decaying governments, which they sometimes dress and turn; but they have nothing to do with those that are firm and substantial. They meet to reform the miscarriages of others; but are commonly prorogued and dissolved for their own when the remedies grow worse than the diseases'.[7]

Few saw the constitutional aggressiveness of the revolutionary parliaments as something to be emulated; few wanted parliament to exchange the advisory and legislative role that it had always had for a more active function in government. But for all its faults, parliament remained, with the law, the badge of England's liberties, the institution that made her constitution so radically different from the despotic monarchies that her people imagined to rule most of continental Europe. The royalist, but deeply constitutionalist Sir Roger Twysden had written, perhaps in the 1650s, that parliaments were 'under God, . . . the greatest preserver of the people's liberty', even if they did need to be 'reduced to the first institution'.[8] Politicians were as intensely sensitive to the effects on the English constitution of the government's actions as was the government to the actions of parliament. As early as 1663, one MP wrote of a rumour 'that there is a design, and an intention to change the constitution of the government of this kingdom and to reduce us after the model of France [where] they have lost all their liberties, and [are] governed by an arbitrary and military power'.[9] By the mid-1670s the notion that some members, at least, of the government were engaged on something more grandiose and more sinister than simply trying to prevent a renewal of Civil War by securing royal power had become well established. Ably summarised by the contemporary poet and pamphleteer Andrew Marvell, and the memorialist Gilbert Burnet, the idea of a government deliberately undermining popular liberties and the constitution would become the standard 'whig' view of the reigns of Charles II and James II.

To later generations, the image of the indolent and hedonistic Charles II as a tyrant has seemed improbable. Modern historians have seen Charles as aiming at nothing more dangerous than preserving the existing rights and powers of the monarchy.[10] James II's interest in extending them, although certainly more seriously pursued, was (it is argued) merely directed towards the achievement of his principal ambition, the revival and firm establishment of Roman Catholicism in England.[11] Certainly, there is little explicit evidence that either king set out expressly to create the 'absolutist' monarchy in England that they undoubtedly admired across the channel, in Louis XIV's France. And there were other reasons, outside the control of the government, which helped to shape distorted public perceptions of what its policies were all about: the success of absolutism in France was one of them; but there was also England's long history of distrust and conflict between Crown and parliament, and the complex interrelationship of religion and politics, which meant that arguments over the repression of nonconformity could easily be turned into arguments about the state's right to coerce religious belief. It was true, too, that some of the government's interest in the maintenance, even extension, of its powers stemmed not from 'absolutist' yearnings, but from a genuine concern about the radical threats to the regime. Certainly the disbanded soldiers of the republican army formed a fearsome radical reserve should a rebellion ever truly take fire; and the government's obsession with the affairs of the sad little band of regicides and republicans forlornly plotting or avoiding each other in exile testifies to the possibility of insurrection.[12]

Yet if there was no grand design for the subjugation of England, both Charles and James were at best casual about the constitution on which their subjects were so sensitive, and often willing to discuss, with their ministers or foreign ambassadors, how to manipulate political or religious anxieties in order to reduce in some way the power of parliament. Early in his reign, Charles conveyed an impression of a king eager to impose his own will on the nation by raising an army.[13] Clarendon sounded warnings about the king's lack of interest in the formal and traditional procedures of law and government by which the country was governed: Charles had 'in his nature so little reverence or esteem for antiquity, and did in truth so much contemn old orders, forms and institutions'; he appointed as his ministers men like Sir Henry Bennet, who 'knew no more of the constitution and laws of England than he did of China, but believed France was the best pattern in the world'. Where his subjects praised antiquity, tradition, and the continuity of law, Charles was 'a great lover of new inventions, and thought [them] the effects of wit and spirit, and fit to control the superstitious observation of the dictates

15

of our ancestors'.[14] James had no great feeling for modernity as such. But as a military man, who surrounded himself with military men, he was instinctively authoritarian. Neither planned an absolutist *coup d'état*, but their autocratic style and their intermittent irritation with the constraints on their government that England's tradition of collaborative government created, explain, and partly justify, the concerns of many contemporaries for the survival of that tradition.

It was perhaps in their other kingdoms, particularly in Scotland, without such sophisticated parliamentary and legal institutions as England possessed, that their autocracy seemed clearer. From 1663 Charles governed in his northern kingdom almost entirely through the Earl of Lauderdale, his secretary of state there: parliamentary opposition to the government's attempts to strengthen its powers and to sort out an ecclesiastical settlement was met with energetic management, and after 1673, parliament's dissolution. Scotland became to some of the English an image of the oppression and savagery of which the Restoration regime was capable. Here, too, however, the conclusion was overblown and partisan. Repression in Scotland was more closely related to religious divisions than to the deliberate blocking of constitutional development; the restoration of episcopacy in 1662 and the deprivation of considerable numbers of Scottish ministers resulted in local, but vigorous opposition, which broke into violence briefly in 1666 and more seriously in 1679. Enforcement of the laws against dissent was entrusted to the military to a far greater extent than it was south of the border, because of the weaknesses of the Scottish system for the execution of justice; if the Scottish authorities resorted to more oppressive and more offensive measures for the control of dissent than did the English – most notoriously of all, the raising of an extra militia in 1678 and quartering it on dissaffected areas – it was as much the result of the inadequacy of the law in Scotland as an attempt to crush the law altogether. Autocracy in Scotland was not an end in itself; but the means through which the Restoration regime tried to establish political control betrayed the ingrained autocratic instincts of its leaders.

The tensions between England's conservatism and legalism, and the impatient authoritarian style of its returning royal family were lost in the general rejoicing of the Restoration. When the Convention's successor, the 'Cavalier Parliament', met in May 1661, the king announced his determination always to consider 'what is a parliament like to think of this action, or of that counsel'.[15] At the time it may not have seemed a strenuous undertaking. The 1661 parliament, elected in the midst of a strong royalist reaction, was notorious for its loyalism. Over half of its members had either themselves fought for the king in the 1640s, had conspired on its behalf in the 1650s, or were the sons of those who had. By the mid-1670s, however, government and parliament were looking at each other with intense suspicion.

Central to their relationship and to its deterioration was finance. It was central, too, to the government's power and independence. The search for financial stability preoccupied Charles and his ministers for most of his reign: in their failure to find it lay the biggest constraint on public policy. Financial weakness had dogged successive governments before the Civil War. Constitutional convention expected the monarch in normal circumstances to pay the expenses of household and government out of his personal revenue – the diminishing profits from the Crown's own lands, the Customs revenue, various feudal taxes, and a few smaller sources. In exceptional circumstances, principally wartime, parliament was expected to open the purses of the monarch's subjects with grants of temporary taxation. Throughout the late sixteenth and early seventeenth centuries, the growing costs of government and the declining revenue from the Crown's estates gradually impoverished the Crown, until it increasingly needed extraordinary grants from parliament to keep it solvent at all. Royal poverty enhanced both the importance of parliament and the ability of those within it to obstruct and confuse government business. But the financial pressure of the Civil War had produced a revolution in government finance: machinery had had to be established capable of equipping and paying an army far larger than any that an English government had assembled before. In 1643 a major new tax, the excise, was introduced; the old fixed-rate subsidy tax was replaced by the assessment which guaranteed the raising of a specific sum; and the old feudal rights of the monarchy, a previously important source of revenue, were abolished.

At the Restoration, the Convention Parliament attempted to create a lasting solution to the problem of royal finance. Its settlement restored part of the old system, but took a good deal from the new. The abolition of the Crown's feudal rights was confirmed: partly in compensation, the Crown was to receive the new excise tax as the Commonwealth regimes had done. The result was a total ordinary revenue of £1.2 million. In comparison with the revenue Charles I had received, it was (in theory at least) a strikingly generous settlement: ordinary revenues in the late 1620s and early 1630s had amounted to only half this sum. Indeed, the grant was based on the expenses of the government in the crisis years of 1637–41, when Charles was forced dramatically to expand his revenues to cope with war in Scotland and a large burden of debt. £1.2 million ought to have covered the government's normal ordinary expenditure. Yet it soon became obvious that the 1660 settlement was much less lavish than it had seemed. Overvaluation of all the revenues meant that the actual revenue fell short of the estimate by almost a third. During 1662 the Cavalier Parliament tried to make up the shortfall with a new tax, on fire hearths, but this brought in less than half the required sum. Despite the enormous efforts of the government to obtain a further addition, the war of 1665–7 and the massive extraordinary sums which were needed as a consequence prevented further discussion of the subject: after the war, despite occasional attempts by the government to reopen the question, parliament never agreed to a further permanent addition to the ordinary revenue. The problem was made worse by the government's expanding commitments and its correspondingly growing expenditure. Charles I had possessed only a very small navy and no army to speak of. His son retained a small army and a considerable navy from the forces built up during the Interregnum. Even in years when these forces were not being employed in major warfare (and in most years the navy was deployed very widely for the protection of English interests) they were extremely expensive: in one of the cheapest, the financial year 1684–5, disbursements to the army amounted to £267,000 and to the navy £481,000.

Such expenses might have been manageable in a revenue that really did amount to £1.2 million. In a revenue that was between two-thirds and three-quarters as much, it left the government with a growing and burdensome debt. Before the beginning of the war of 1665–7, its debt already amounted to £1.25 million; by 1670 it had stretched to about £3 million. Despite frequent efforts to reduce government expenditure and a moratorium on some debt repayments – the 'Stop of the Exchequer' – in 1672, the debt was still £2.4 million in 1679. The inefficiency of the London money market made it difficult, too, for the government to raise further finance in a crisis. Successive lord treasurers and treasury commissions sought a variety of solutions to the government's financial dilemma, and tried by all possible expedients to head off the bankruptcy that threatened whenever the government became embroiled in any more than ordinary expenditure.[16]

The most obvious means was to appeal to parliament. After the grant of the hearth tax in 1662 the suspicions of some members of parliament that further additions to the permanent revenue were required simply to render future extraordinary grants – and hence parliament itself – unnecessary helped to defeat any attempts in that direction.[17] Temporary additions to Crown revenues were more acceptable. In 1668 additional excise duties, and in 1670 additional customs duties were granted, which supplemented Crown revenue until 1678. There were the extraordinary grants as well. Most of the extraordinary taxation granted by parliament in the 1660s and 1670s went to pay for wars: £5 million altogether for the 1665–7 war against the Dutch; £1.18 million for the 1672–4 war; and the Poll Tax of 1678 designed to raise troops for war against France. Some more grants were made for other military purposes: for paying off the army and navy in 1660;

for strengthening the fleet in 1671 and 1677; and the disbandment of the army in 1678 and 1679. Several others, however, went to help balance the Crown's ordinary accounts. In 1661 the enormous sum of £1.2 million was given to help the Crown pay off some of the burden of debt it had inherited from the Commonwealth; subsidies in 1663 and 1671 were intended to fill the gap in the ordinary revenue.

The government could try, too, to improve the yield of the normal revenue. Successive lord treasurers and treasury commissions were energetic and dedicated in seeking new, better ways of tax collection. The managers of the court's finances could attempt to reduce expenditure, though the ease with which the king would let himself be prevailed upon to grant away lucrative sources of revenue made 'retrenchment' a difficult art. Treasury regimes constantly tried to impose some sort of central control over departmental spending, with varying degrees of success: but the expenditure of the royal household itself defeated them all.

Occasional windfalls, such as the dowry brought by the king's marriage in 1662, temporarily boosted Crown revenues, but sometimes the prospect of profit encouraged the government into ill-advised projects: both wars with the Dutch were defended in part with the claim that they would bring in prize money worth more to the treasury than they cost it. The Crown's participation in major trading projects such as the Royal African Company of 1663 may have been prompted by the belief that they might contribute to the government's finances. In 1662 the government sold Dunkirk, captured by English troops in 1658, to the French: an action which, however financially sensible, was deeply unpopular. Criticisms of some of the government's other expedients, however, had much greater force. The moratorium on some debt repayments in 1672, caused by the scarcity of government funds to wage war with the Dutch and in part by the weakness of a system for attracting credit which had been created in 1665, could perhaps not have been avoided, even though it showed to potential lenders that the government could not be trusted to repay their money unless it was backed by firm statutory guarantees. The resort to the French government for financial subsidies, begun in the 1670s as the result of treaties between Louis XIV and Charles II, placed the king in the demeaning position of one of Louis' many European clients, and ended up with Charles surrendering a good deal of his freedom of political movement – especially when, later in the 1670s, Louis was subsidising Charles simply in order to keep him out of the European conflict altogether. The sum involved was not large – England received £746,000 from France during the course of the 1670s – and Charles in any case had his own reasons for wanting an alliance. Yet the price in terms of his relationship with his parliament and his people was enormous.[18]

By resorting to such expedients, the government's accounts could be made finally to balance: yet it was perpetually short of money, and even at the end of the reign a mountain of debt remained. Crises in the Crown's finances occurred regularly, and were especially severe when war inflated expenditure and cut customs revenue: at the end of the war of 1665–7 the government was effectively bankrupt, and one minster wrote to another that it could 'moulder to nothing in a short time under the weight of its necessities'.[19] Not until the 1690s, under the pressure of constant war, would there develop the sort of system of government finance and credit which could cope with the demands placed upon it; and not until the mid-1680s would the court exercise the sort of economy and discipline in its expenditure needed to bring the government within its means. Even then, it was a dramatic boom in trade, raising the customs and excise revenues, that was principally responsible for the improvement in royal finances from 1681 onwards.

For the moment, parliament was intensely, and often justifiably, suspicious of the extravagance and corruption of government. As early as 1663 MPs criticised the granting away of Crown lands to courtiers; during the 1665–7 war their concern grew as the vast sums they had granted seemed to disappear to nowhere. A satire of 1668 described how the commons 'Too late grown wise, they their treasure see,/ Consum'd by fraud or lost by treachery'.[20] Taking their cue from the government's offer in 1661 to open royal accounts to parliament, some of the stronger of the government's critics proposed a parliamentary committee of accounts in 1666; and at the end of 1667 the court had to accept a parliamentary commission to examine its accounts. It was originally at the government's motion that clauses were added in some money bills determining the method in which the money should be disbursed – the 1665 assessment bill contained such a clause, in a scheme designed to help in raising credit. But it soon became a device of the government's critics, in order to prevent the diversion of money granted for a particular purpose to another. 'Appropriation' clauses were added to the assessment bill of 1667, and proposed to money bills in 1668 and 1671. By the late 1670s most of the money bills which were passed contained them.[21]

The use of appropriation clauses and the extension of parliamentary oversight of the revenue did not originate in deliberate efforts to expand the power of the legislature. Yet they do indicate the way in which the government's financial weakness laid it open to exploitation by men in parliament who either sincerely or insincerely opposed government measures: courtiers hoping to oust their rivals as ministers, interest groups, and those who saw themselves as the guardians of popular liberties. Almost any measure the government took to resolve its financial problems – even severe domestic economy, which reduced the number and value of jobs and perquisites that could be offered to courtiers – could have the effect of increasing its critics' effectiveness, their grievances, or their suspicions. The Crown's financial inadequacies were not only the battleground for many of the political conflicts of the reign, they were also, in one sense, their cause.

They also limited the government's ability to restrict the role of parliament. Right at the beginning of the reign, it took steps to do so in theory. When in 1661 and 1662 some of the regicides were put on trial, the government used the proceedings to mount a strong attack on the proposition that the Lords and Commons shared sovereignty with the Crown, an argument that was also deliberately rejected in the preamble to the Militia Act passed in 1661: control of the armed forces, one of the classic marks of sovereignty, had to be unambiguously in government hands.[22] Restricting it in practice was approached more gingerly. The 1641 Triennial Act, accepted by Charles I as one of the last bills passed before his final break with parliament, made mandatory the calling of parliament once every three years, and removed much of the Crown's freedom to summon or dismiss it at will. The Act was, claimed the solicitor general, 'dethroning the king by Act of Parliament'. In 1664, after much hesitation, the government decided to press for its removal, replacing it with a bill which, though still stipulating that parliament should meet at least every three years, specified no machinery to enforce the requirement. In the following debate, government speakers put their view of the proper role of parliaments: they were 'the physic of the nation, not the food', said one, 'to be summoned but in time of sickness and want of help in affairs, not at any fixed periods'. A more liberal version of parliament's role still existed, however: one of the other speakers in the debate, the distinguished lawyer John Vaughan, claimed that a right to *annual* parliaments had been established in the Middle Ages, and that frequent sessions gave the people some protection against the abuses and corruptions of government. But most members accepted the government's argument, and their conservatism was clear in the repetition of the claim that in the 1640s the expansion of parliament had ended in the horror and confusion of civil war and regicide: to tinker with one part of the constitution was to risk destroying the whole.[23]

All assertions of the formally subordinate status of parliament, however, were increasingly at odds with the informal reality in which the government's financial problems resulted. Parliament's dominance of the political scene during the 1660s and 1670s provided an almost permanent forum for the articulation of the grievances of the country. The consequent concentration of criticism and political conflict encouraged its rapid development and sophistication. Historians have rightly abandoned the term 'opposition' as applied to the critics of government in pre-eighteenth-century parliaments. Governments were opposed on different issues by different groups for different reasons: often those opposing them were themselves prominent office-holders. Yet it remains true that a few influential and respected members of either house could easily become the leaders of and spokesmen for widely felt unease or resentment within parliament, and that they often co-operated with one another in order to press the government as hard as possible. By 1666 or 1667 it was common to refer to 'court' and 'country' parties within parliament. The labels may not have meant a great deal in terms of organisation or party discipline, but they were symbolic of alienation from the government and the existence of a core of critics.[24]

Early on in the Cavalier Parliament a kernel of opposition to the government's constitutional and security measures was established, including both independent-minded former royalists, and those whose concern for the rights of the subject against the machinations of the court dated back at least to their opposition to Charles I's government in the early years of the Long Parliament. Among the first was John Vaughan, a close friend of the former parliamentarian legal theorist John Selden; among the second was the now elderly Denzil, Lord Holles, one of the five members whose arrest Charles I had demanded in 1641. Other leading opponents of government policy could come from within the court, from men whose ambition and resentment of their colleagues could be mixed with dislike of particular policies to make them particularly effective thorns in the court's side. Playing on the sentiments of the members, court factions accused their rivals in power and policy of pro-catholic leanings, corruption, or advising the king to assume arbitrary power. In 1663 the Earl of Bristol attempted to impeach the Earl of Clarendon; in 1667 Clarendon was impeached, partly at the instigation of the Duke of Buckingham, and from 1668 to 1672 a collection of ministers – christened the 'cabal' not because they possessed a common purpose, nor because they worked excessively secretly, but because the initial letters of their names happened to spell the word – struggled for pre-eminent power, poisoning both government and parliament in the process. Such leaders, whatever their intentions, vied and sometimes co-operated to gain the attention of more than 600 confused and often politically unsophisticated members: when they succeeded, they could block supply and legislation and exert considerable pressure on the king and his ministers.[25]

Their existence and the government's penury made the court's own efforts to render parliament more manageable an increasing preoccupation. Yet 'management', as the court had found as long ago as 1614, could exacerbate the problem it was designed to solve. Government interference with the independence of parliament struck at the heart of its power, and members were quick to attack anything which seemed to carry the risk of its decline into ineffectiveness. Nevertheless, in the 1660s and 1670s that interference grew rapidly; members protested as they saw government corruption spreading into parliament. In the early 1660s government management had been limited to the informal methods in use a century before: the government's wishes would be communicated to a small number of members, some privy councillors and other influential speakers often tied to the government by no more than hopes of preferment or family connexions. It was common, however, for ministers competing for policy and power to cultivate their own following within parliament. In a government whose attention was more and more directed to parliament, ministers and courtiers recognised how the possession of a faction in parliament added to their influence at court. In 1677 Andrew Marvell complained that once elected, MPs 'list themselves straightway into some court faction, and it is as well known among them, to what Lord each of them retain, as when formerly they wore coats, and badges'.[26] In the mid-1660s Sir Henry Bennet built up his own group of followers in the commons; already in 1663 he was able to mount a challenge to Clarendon's control of the court's parliamentary programme. By the end of the decade his use of the jobs and benefits within his gift as secretary of state in order to expand his parliamentary faction was being condemned as a scandal – although those who condemned it in the 1669 satire *The Alarum* may well have been members of another faction led by the Duke of Buckingham.[27]

In 1672, the advent of war against the Dutch, a declaration granting toleration to nonconformists from the Church of England, and the Stop of the Exchequer, coupled with the growing realisation that the heir to the throne had become a Roman Catholic, began to turn the political atmosphere icy. From 1673 the new lord treasurer, the Earl of Danby, tried to cope with the growth in parliamentary discontent by expanding further the numbers of MPs receiving from the government pensions and gifts, promises of title, jobs, and local offices. In 1676 he claimed to have secured the votes of about 250 members. Yet Danby's methods, regarded with revulsion by 'country' members, and by a few in the court as well, were never very successful: the bait was in many cases small and not very tempting, and members were subject to other pressures, from their constituencies and friends, even their consciences. Such success as Danby had was as much due to his espousal of anglican royalist values and policies as to his capacity for bribery. Even so, to many parliamentarians Danby's activities not only showed the government's disregard for the constitution that they held dear, but they were also the first step in the destruction of parliament and the introduction of arbitrary government. A parliament which had begun in 1661 full of royalism and the orthodox sentiment that England was best served when king and parliament were most united had begun to suspect the government of holding an entirely different idea of what that unity meant.[28]

For many historians in the past, the institutional conflict of parliament and government was merely a symptom of deeper conflicts and concerns. Parliament's growth in power during the Civil War and its attempt to retain it after the Restoration were a reflection (it has been argued) of the increasing political and economic dominance of the gentry. Historians recognise that the Interregnum gave the higher gentry a considerable shock: they were displaced from their positions in local administration by the smaller, 'parish' gentry, by some whom they would barely call gentlemen, and by a few whom they definitely would not. At the Restoration, the grander gentry naturally reassumed their old role in local government. But many historians have claimed that they did more, and tightened their control in national and local affairs, gradually excluding the central government altogether. Their hegemony confirmed and strengthened by the Revolution of 1688, they passed on to their eighteenth-century heirs the serene assurance of a ruling class which had tamed both the government and its social inferiors. The Restoration, S. K. Roberts has most recently argued, was 'a surrender to the country gentry'.[29]

Undoubtedly, many of the institutions through which pre-Civil War governments had exercised close supervision of the work of local administrators had been either abolished or enfeebled. Star Chamber, the quasi-judicial court through which privy councillors called many of them to account, had been abolished in a statute of 1641, as had its sister regional courts based at York and in Ludlow. Though the government toyed with their recreation, only the Council of the Marches of Wales, at Ludlow, was restored, and that only in an attenuated form.[30] It is true, too, that statutes of the Restoration period – particularly the new Poor Law and the Militia statutes – added more to the gentry's already large responsibilities for the government of their communities. Nevertheless, throughout the 1660s and 1670s many of the gentry believed that the depression and the 'decay of rents' threatened to destroy the economic basis of their power. The government, in any case, had other means of exercising its control of the gentry's local administration. The privy council itself took a close interest in their affairs; by the 1670s the government was regularly altering, for political reasons, the personnel of the commissions of the peace.[31] Few of the gentry wished to exclude the central government from local affairs: indeed, partisan struggles within local communities meant that, if anything, the government was more often appealed to to resolve disputes than before. The relationship between government and gentry was after all not one of competition, but of mutual advantage: the government got a class of unpaid royal servants who could be relied on to keep peace and order throughout the country; the gentry received in return honours and offices and the influence at court which helped them to benefit their local communities. The gentry were the mediators between Crown and people, 'the fence which keeps distance between the king and the vulgarity'.[32] It was a relationship which had its tensions: the gentry could be jealous and protective of their local power, while governments might be unhappy about relying too far on their uncertain motivation and abilities as well as irritated by the local feuds into which they were constantly being dragged. But it was not a relationship which the gentry, at least, wished fundamentally to alter by taking more direct and personal control of aspects of local government. On the contrary, they felt deeply the need to strengthen it in the face of threats to their social dominance.

The greatest fear was not of government encroachment, but of social subversion and the government's betrayal of its special relationship with the gentry. The Civil War had jolted never very secure assumptions about the permanence of the social order, and government and gentry had joined forces to protect themselves from the terror of popular attempts to influence politics: an 'Act against tumults and disorders', designed to prevent popular pressure being used to intimidate parliament, was the first act passed by the Cavalier Parliament. The gentry's desire to reassert their control in the country was reflected in the passage of a series of harsh laws, protecting their hunting rights from poaching, the first of which was passed in 1671; equally it informed their attitude to religious dissent, which they regarded as evidence of a contempt of authority among the common people: 'Blind as the cyclops, and as wild as he,/ They owned a lawless savage liberty', wrote Dryden of them during the Civil War. 'There is a spirit of grudging and opposition lurking in the breasts of most clowns', wrote one Bristol gentleman in 1674, 'and no doubt they watch and hope for a time to pull them down, and to take their pleasure of a sweet and full revenge upon them.'[33]

The more sophisticated challenge seemed to come from the new wealth of the City, and here the government's response was disquietingly ambivalent. From the 1660s, as prices of agricultural products fell and rents fell with them, the gentry's prejudice against the moneyed wealth of the City grew ever stronger. More and more beholden to the City themselves for finance to cover their expenses or improve their land, they resented wealth built out of their own difficulties at what they considered to be exorbitant rates of interest. Royalists particularly blamed the bankers, whom they felt to have had a large hand in the exploitation of royalist estates during the war. The City was (however inaccurately) depicted as dominated by presbyterians, whose reputation for pious words mixed with sharp practice accorded well with the gentry's view of the City as a whole. The gentry, it seemed to them, were impoverished as the City got rich. Eventually, some of them felt, their power and influence would go the same way as their wealth. Bankers, said one MP in 1670, 'are the commonwealths-men that destroy the nobility and gentry'; they were parasites feeding off, and gradually killing, the wealth and power of the gentry.[34]

The persistent fear that the country gentry's wealth and influence were in terminal decline pervaded Restoration politics. The king and court were anxiously watched for signs that they might be withdrawing their confidence from useless, declining gentlemen. There were rumours in 1667 that one of the king's more offensive courtiers had urged him to 'crush the English gentlemen, saying that £300 a year was enough for any man', and that Clarendon had denied that 'three or four hundred country gentlemen [in parliament] could either be prudent men or statesmen'.[35] The gentry bitterly attacked the court's corruption through which money and the arts of royal favour could bring others the valued profits and prominence of office, while they, the natural rulers of the country and the proper advisers of the king, were ignored and snubbed. If the gentry were no longer regarded at court and no longer respected in the country, their power, and their role as the mediators of power between both, was unlikely to last long.

Up to a point their suspicions were justified, although the government was as yet far from becoming especially attuned to the moneyed interest, and there were no viable alternatives to the enforcement of order through the local commissions of the peace. But however much some ministers – particularly Clarendon and the Earl of Southampton, lord treasurer from 1660 to 1667 – may have sympathised with the gentry's own view of their role in government, there were pressures on the government which were forcing it to become more centralised and more professional. The Civil War had shown that the gentry's support for the Crown might always be conditional and would rarely be total; and it was quite obvious that their administrative sophistication and commitment to the business of ruling were not always sufficient to meet the increasingly complex demands of government.

These pressures were most deeply felt – because the subject was so close to the government's heart – in the arrangements for the country's defence. Government and gentry were agreed at the Restoration on the necessity of getting rid of the remnants of the Interregnum army, whose power, and the extent to which it still contained radical, anti-monarchical elements, threatened the monarchy's existence. Its peaceful disbandment at the end of 1660 and in early 1661 was greeted with relief by gentry and government alike. The Interregnum had given England her first experience of a standing professional army and an unpleasant instance of how an unpopular government could be maintained in power by force alone. Its use during the 1650s in local administration had shown how military force could displace the gentry in governing their local communities, eroding their national and local importance. The gentry were delighted to see that threat, at least, recede; but they looked on unhappily at the government's interest in creating its own army. As Roger L'Estrange pleaded, in 1662, 'that prince is great, safe and happy, that commands by his arms abroad and governs by his laws at home . . . Good laws and good officers, will do the business without an army'.[36] To create an army, conservatives stressed, was to bring an unpredictable and violent bull into the china shop of the English constitution. Even those who created it might find it turn against them (as the army had against the

Long Parliament). More than anything else, it was likely to destroy the tranquil rule of law that the gentry demanded.

The militia represented no such dangers. Raised locally, assembled when necessary, and mustered and exercised a few times a year, it was firmly under the control of the local gentry. As an army, it was almost useless, as its performance during Dutch landings in 1667 or Monmouth's rebellion in 1685 showed. Nevertheless, the gentry persisted in regarding it not only as an essential guarantee of English liberties but also (with reform) as a potentially sufficient fighting force. In legislation of 1662 and 1663 – based partly on an ordinance of the Rump Parliament in 1659 – the confused mass of law and prerogative that related to the militia was codified and a tax was created which could be used to pay its soldiers when it was called out. These reforms brought some improvement in its efficiency; even so, its performance was variable. In some counties keen local gentlemen closely interested themselves in its organisation and training; in others it was badly neglected.[37]

Though the militia reforms added to the responsibilities, and hence the power, that the gentry exercised in the country, they were prompted by a concern that the government was more interested in professional than amateur solutions to the problem of defence. Always in fear of armed insurrection, even in 1660 Charles was eager to establish some form of professional military force. The brief but bloody rising of a handful of religious fanatics in London in January 1661 showed up the inadequacy of the militia. Immediately, the government began to create a small army out of the more reliable soldiers from the disbanded commonwealth army, and kept other units together by sending them to garrison its possessions of Dunkirk and Tangier and to support Portugal in its war against Spain. In England, Charles kept a permanent force of about 3000 or 4000, besides which there were armies in Scotland and Ireland of about 2700 and 7500 respectively, although the political complexion of the latter was such that the government never cared to rely on it.[38] It was minute in comparison to the armies on the continent: by

1675 Louis XIV's army had been expanded to about 100,000; the English army of the Interregnum had amounted at its peak to almost 60,000 men. The gentry's affection for the militia did not rule out acceptance of an army the size of Charles's, however: they, after all, were as concerned as the government about the possibility of popular rebellion, and many welcomed the security a small force based mainly in the cities and the towns could give, without threatening a wider control over the country. Yet they were always suspicious of any addition to the army's numbers or its role. In peacetime, the few soldiers quartered in a handful of garrison towns caused little objection: soldiers and civilians could get on even amicably, and commanding officers were often welcomed into local administration. But when the army was rapidly expanded in wartime or at times of great political tension it became more difficult for military and civilian to live easily beside one another: the pressure on accommodation forced the army to quarter soldiers on private individuals; and large numbers of troops moving around the country could leave a trail of damage, robbery and outrage in their wake.[38]

Anxieties that rule by military force might ultimately replace government by co-operation and consent were aroused each time the army was expanded to meet some emergency. Temporary regiments were raised in 1662, to help enforce the Act of Uniformity, in 1667, in anticipation of a Dutch invasion; in 1672 for war with the Dutch, and in 1678, in expectation of war with France. In 1667 there were wide-spread rumours that the purpose of the expansion was 'to govern by a standing army'. There was a strong – and not entirely inaccurate – belief in the existence of a number of men within the government, including the Duke of York, who pressed for the use of the army as a regular instrument of domestic policy. The expansion of the army in 1673 for the war with the Dutch brought out fears of the insidious ways in which the military could corrupt the nation: as Sir Thomas Meres complained in parliament

> it brings in the billeting of soldiers, against the Petition of Right.
> . . . You are told also of martial law, made for the governing

these men, against all the laws of England. Martial law has arbitrary principles and arbitrary power – we like not these arbitrary principles in any councils – this army has the youth of the nation; it debauches them, and fills them with such principles.[39]

Already, the army was seen as an instrument of arbitrary power; as fears of the influence of popery in government rose in the 1670s after the conversion of the Duke of York it came to be seen as an instrument of catholicism as well. Catholic officers in the army were seen as ominous evidence of a planned catholic coup.[40] When the war ended in 1674, most of the new regiments were disbanded. In early 1678, however, responding to popular pressure, the government raised a large army, of about 28,000, in order to help defend the Netherlands against France. The purpose was a fairly popular one, but so rapid and so sudden an expansion of the army was alarming, particularly when its instigator – the Earl of Danby – was already widely suspected of planning to undermine parliament. When the Dutch accepted peace before most of the soldiers could arrive in Flanders, the suspicion grew stronger: and when uncertainty over peace terms made the government refuse for the moment to disband the troops, the disagreement became acrimonious. When peace was finally signed, the government demanded more money for their disbandment. If the money was refused, some wondered, would it be raised without consent, by the army itself?

In this case, the charge against the government was a little unfair, since it was plainly the difficulty of international negotiation that was the main cause of the delay in the new regiments' disbandment, not ambitions to retain them. But while it may never have placed at the centre of its strategy a coup to replace rule by law with rule by the army there can be little doubt that there were many within the government – York in particular – who found the idea of a larger force attractive and would have liked to expand it. The court in 1662 attempted to find some financial basis for a larger semi-permanent army, and the idea was often floated, particularly during the discussions for a treaty with France in 1669–70, of strengthening the army in order to encourage parliament to be rather more amenable.[41] Danby in 1677 expressed a wish for 'some small insurrection' which might allow the government to get 'into some condition of arms and money by the consent of the people, who would otherwise not give the one and be jealous of the other'.[42]

There was never any prospect of altering the system of local government by the gentry through commissions of the peace. Even if it had wanted to, the government would never have had the resources to do so; nevertheless, the government was always concerned about the reliability of local administration. It was difficult to place full reliance on the gentry when many of them were themselves politically suspect, through participation in the rebellion, or through their nonconformity from the Church of England. How could the monarchy feel itself securely in control when it doubted the loyalty of so many of its local governors? In the interests of harmony, the government at first put the thought aside: the appointments of Justices of the Peace made in 1660 were of the most prominent leaders of their communities, virtually irrespective of past politics. Those of more modest origins, often appointed to the commissions of the peace during the Interregnum, were removed but many appointees of the 1650s remained – in Hampshire, 36 per cent of them.[43] Yet the government could scarcely ignore the distinction between those who had fought against the king or had done nothing to help him, and those who had actively shown their support for the monarchy over the past twenty years, particularly whenever the government was anxious to ensure the enforcement of pieces of controversial religious legislation. In 1670, the government abandoned its policy of creating broadly based commissions of the peace when it purged from the lists the opponents of the Conventicle Act against dissenters; in the later 1670s political purges became more common, as Danby engineered an anglican royalist reaction against dissent. These were not yet on the scale of the purges that were to follow in the 1680s, but the local feud that followed the removal in 1676 of the lord lieutenant of Norfolk, Lord Townshend, a former presbyterian, and his replacement with a man of impeccable anglican royalist credentials was nevertheless a clear indication of how profoundly they could alienate and irritate the gentry.[44]

Strengthening royal control over the towns was rather simpler, although there the problem of unreliable local governors was more acute, for they were often run by oligarchic, self-perpetuating corporations. To ministers, such corporations could be nurseries of sedition in which former parliamentarians, supporters of the Protectorate and dissenters, ousted from power at national level, managed to retain shreds of it in their little local territories. Many anglican royalists concurred. When a bill empowering commissioners to remove the disaffected members of corporations and restore royalists ejected during the Interregnum was read in the Commons in 1661 it was the work of anglican royalists determined to clear their enemies out of local government. But the court took the opportunity to try to introduce a more lasting control over town corporations. Amendments made in the Lords, probably on the government's initiative, made the bill into a strong assault on municipal independence, giving the Crown power to change the borough charters which conferred the corporations' privileges, reserving to itself in the new ones the power to appoint or approve its principal officers. Such an extension of government powers over corporations was seen as intolerable. The gentry may have had no love for town oligarchies, but many of them themselves sat in parliament as the representatives of such boroughs, and Crown interference in what at best was a fairly close relationship was as much to be resisted as interference by the military in their running of their counties. The government had to concede, and the bill remained rather more limited in scope. The enforcement of the Corporation Act in 1662–3 did lead to quite extensive changes in the membership of town corporations: in some towns a majority was displaced. But a lack of suitable replacements, and the tendency of the displaced to find their way back reduced its ultimate effectiveness. The government continued, discreetly, to try to extend its powers in town governments: in a number of subsequent renewals of borough charters it was careful to insert powers to approve the appointments of some borough officials, and even – in the case of Gloucester in 1672 – power to remove at will any member of the corporation.[45]

The Corporation Act showed that there were conflicts within the gentry that were much deeper than, and to some extent lay beneath, those between the gentry and the government. At the Restoration many of the gentry tried to assume that the political and social unity of county society could be restored. Yet their efforts could scarcely conceal the fact that before 1660, and especially before 1649, county society had in many cases been deeply divided. The deep commitment that many still retained to the causes for which they had fought could induce powerful strains within local communities. The Act of Oblivion and Indemnity, passed by the Convention and confirmed by the Cavalier Parliament was seen (by the government) as central to political stability: its injunction that 'all names and terms of distinction' be 'put into utter oblivion' was backed by penalties for those who in malice taunted their old enemies with 'any name or names, or other word of reproach, anyway tending to revive the memory of the late differences or the occasions thereof'. But the penalties were small and ineffective. When Colonel Edward Harley, an old parliamentarian soldier, was called a traitor and rebel by a junior royalist officer, he was dissuaded from prosecution by his royalist neighbours. Only one prosecution is known to have been made under the Act, even though old parliamentarians were frequently harassed by vengeful or nervous royalist gentry. Many royalists found the very idea of consigning their past sufferings to oblivion offensive, and took pains to ensure that their memory was kept alive.[46]

While the Act of Oblivion may have been ineffective, it and the Act confirming judicial proceedings in the Interregnum were deeply resented by royalists. In the 1640s and 1650s they had suffered heavily from the sequestration and sometimes confiscation of their estates and from discriminatory taxation. Many had been forced to sell land, or confirm the sale of confiscated land in return for cash payments. At the Restoration, land which had been confiscated and sold, but where the sale had not been confirmed, could be recovered. But where the sale had been confirmed by the vendor, or where the land had been sold simply to raise money to meet discriminatory taxation, the Acts of Oblivion and Judicial Proceedings effectively protected the purchaser. Few royalist families were permanently ruined by the effects of the Civil War – in those that claimed to have been, the war had usually simply hastened an existing decline. But the war did impose great hardship and penury on many of those accustomed to a position at the head of society, and it seemed to them that, once restored to that position, they were unable to retaliate against their former oppressors who had profited from their plight. The failure quickly to put in place a system of compensation for royalist soldiers wounded in the war invited unfortunate comparisons with the efficiency and speed with which the Commonwealth army was paid off.[47]

Few royalists felt they found justice either when the government began to distribute offices. The deepest resentment was caused by the government's willingness to take into office some of those who a few years before had been fighting against the royal cause. Anxious to obtain support as broadly based as possible in the early years of the Restoration, the government placed important positions in the hands of able and politically influential representatives of what it called the 'presbyterian interest'. As a result old parliamentarians were strikingly prominent in high office: the Duke of Albemarle as captain-general of the army, the Earl of Manchester as lord chamberlain, Lord Ashley (later the Earl of Shaftesbury) as chancellor of the exchequer, and there were many others. For royalists, to place trust in old rebels while passing over those who had already proved their loyalty was incomprehensible, an invitation to anti-monarchist conspiracy. It is clear that the charges of favouritism to old parliamentarians were much exaggerated. Those whom the government really trusted, who filled the second-rank offices and were in effective control of the execution of policy, were overwhelmingly anglican royalists. It is clear, too, that the government's difficulty in attempting to reward its former supporters lay less in the fact that so many former parliamentarians had been compensated as in the fact that there were simply too few offices in the government's gift and too little money for pensions to go round. But such arguments did not mollify the royalists. For them, it was more than a question of financial reward. If former presbyterians and parliamentarians held some of the principal offices of state, they possessed in their hands a large proportion of the government's patronage. By its judicious exercise, they could introduce other members of their party into government. Royalists could be gradually excluded altogether, and their power and influence both with the king and in the country at large would wither away. Presbyterians were especially odious. They had worked for the Restoration, claimed royalists, only because the power of religious radicals made them alarmed for the safety of their own power. They were regarded as hypocrites who pretended to political and religious principle but had no more in their hearts than their own advancement. Their supple consciences, the wealth they had built up in the Civil War, and the government's anxiety to please them would, royalists bitterly reflected, soon allow them entirely to capture royal favour. Some royalists, like the journalist Roger L'Estrange, saw it as deeply sinister: 'what can these people mean then, but mischief to the king, whose business 'tis further to ruin those, that are already undone for serving him?'[48]

For the rest of the period, anglican royalists, both in central and local government, tried to hold on to power and influence against what they saw as presbyterian efforts to capture office and political control. They pleaded with the king and the government to rely on them. One of them told Secretary Williamson in December 1669 that:

> the king could not do himself greater right than to declare he would rely upon those who in the worst of times never swerved from him but with the hazard of their lives [and] the ruin of their estates, maintained his title ... [but] those who were forward to serve all powers would be faithful to none.[49]

Throughout the period royalists tried to secure themselves more firmly in power, in town corporations, local commissions of the peace and in the central administration, wresting power from the old Cromwellians, old parliamentarians and nonconformists wherever they had succeeded in retaining it. Not always did they find the government responsive to their desires: in the early 1660s, it had sought to play down old political conflicts by insisting on the Act of Indemnity. Clarendon's fall, in 1667, added to the power of those whom royalists regarded with distaste and resentment: amongst the principals were the future Earl of Shaftesbury, a former Cromwellian, and the Duke of Buckingham, whose closeness to presbyterian and Cromwellian circles was well known. But the administration of the Earl of Danby, from about 1674, played systematically on cavalier prejudices. 'If . . . there can be any way contrived', wrote one of Danby's political advisers, Sir Robert Wiseman, in 1676,

> that the cavalier party may be convinced that the king loves them more than any sort of men, that their affections may be revived, and that the whole party once more may be cheerfully united and knit together, it will be a day more advantageous to the king than if he had an alliance with the most powerful prince alive.[50]

For all the public rejoicing of the Restoration, the Civil War had left deep divisions in political society. Welcoming their return to amity in their rhetoric, the government, the gentry and the parties of the Civil War nevertheless all remained wary of each other. Insecure in their power, or uncertain of the peace, all watched anxiously for how the others would behave, and set to work to rebuild and extend their defences against the storms that still might come. In the process the conflicts and tensions of the war were passed on, in suspicion and mistrust, to another generation.

3

CONFLICTS OF CONSCIENCE

Much of the heat in Restoration politics was generated by religious argument. Purely theological issues, it is true, were no longer as great an element in political conflict as they had been before the Civil War; Sir Peter Pett claimed in 1681 that 'the old way of arguing about speculative points in religion with passion and loudness . . . is grown out of use, and a gentlemanly temper that men use in debating natural experiments has succeeded in its room'.[1] But the religious disputes of the Restoration were not principally over questions of salvation: they involved many of the deepest issues and anxieties of seventeenth-century, and particularly post-Civil War, England – the political effects of a diversity of religious belief; the security of the law; partisan animosity; social antagonism; and national identity.

Religion had been the most potent ingredient in the final division into royalist and parliamentarian which had finally brought the Civil War: it was, wrote the puritan divine Richard Baxter, 'principally the differences about religious matters that filled up the parliament's armies, and put the resolution and valour into their soldiers, which carried them on in another manner than mercenary soldiers are carried on'.[2] Even such a cynic as the satirist Samuel Butler said that religion was what the combatants thought they were fighting for:

> When Civil fury first grew high,
> And men fell out they knew not why;

When hard words, Jealousies and Fears
Set Folks together by the ears,
And made them fight, like mad or drunk
For Dame Religion as for Punk,
Whose honesty they all durst swear for,
Though not a man of them knew wherefore.[3]

In the 1640s, as radical puritans and Scottish presbyterians forced unacceptable ministers from their livings, bishops from their sees, and cathedral clergy from their chapters, the Church of England began to disintegrate. The Church's Prayer Book was replaced as the official liturgy with a presbyterian formulary. Presbyterians, though, never succeeded in imposing their will on the country at large: no national Church effectively replaced the old anglican system; each parish came to be effectively autonomous in matters of worship and ecclesiastical discipline, reflecting a wide range of religious opinion. The weakness of presbyterian power at national level brought an even greater diversity of religious opinions: 'independent' congregations, baptists, fifth monarchists and quakers flourished. Horrified by the execution of the king, alarmed by the religious and political radicalism of many of the sects that had sprung up, many presbyterians worked for a royal restoration: Monck's intervention in 1659 may have been motivated by fears that religious radicals were on the verge of capturing real political power. With the return of the excluded members, a restoration of the monarchy was not in doubt; yet the future of the Church was an enormous problem for the government to sort out. Would presbyterian prominence in restoring the king result in the creation of a presbyterian Church? Or would anglicans, who had throughout the Interregnum refused to compromise the integrity of their Church's liturgy and doctrine, be able to re-establish the Church of England's hegemony?

Those whom their enemies called 'presbyterians' were the heirs of the pre-war puritans, and the name – rejected by some, accepted by others – stood for a wide variety of doctrinal and ceremonial positions. On one side, the most

41

moderate presbyterians differed little from anglicans except in their desire for a less hierarchical episcopate, and a rather more severe purge of the vestiges of Roman Catholicism from the Church's ceremonial. On the other, extreme presbyterians hoped for a much more calvinistic slant to the Church's doctrine and the sort of national organisation by ministers and elders that the Scottish and the continental reformed Churches possessed. Moderates were strongly attached to the notion of a single national church, and prepared, therefore, to give their allegiance to the Church of England if it was a little modified; extremists were willing, if necessary, to separate altogether from the national church in order to worship in a more acceptable environment. Whatever their divisions, the presbyterians' role in bringing about the Restoration, as well as the government's estimate of the extent of their support (particularly among the gentry) demanded that their wishes be taken seriously.

Both presbyterians and anglicans took the smaller sects, though not their wishes, extremely seriously. In 1666 the French ambassador estimated that there were 60 different religious sects in England; in 1681 the royalist propagandist Roger L'Estrange put the number at 170. They varied from 'independents' – little different from presbyterians in their calvinistic theology, but antipathetic to any national ecclesiastical system – to far more exotic groups. A majority of baptists, who stressed baptism of adult believers as the basis of the fellowship of a gathered Church, remained fairly calvinistic in theology, although a large number had rejected a predestinarian for an 'arminian' belief in the potential salvation of all. Quakers went further, drawing their beliefs from a *mélange* of radical protestantism: they rejected predestination and the Trinity and the corruption of all worldly churches and possessed a strong vein of mysticism, claiming for themselves divine inspiration which transcended the instruction of the scriptures. These sects could claim large numbers of adherents; by 1660 there were perhaps between 35,000 and 60,000 Quakers and 25,000 or so Baptists. Other sects were small, most tiny. Many clergy – anglican and presbyterian – were outraged by their outlandish theology; laymen as well were disturbed by their evangelism and lively contempt for the traditional ecclesiastical system; but most disturbing was their extreme social and political radicalism. The quakers challenged assumptions of order and hierarchy: the nobility and gentry were founded, one of them claimed, on 'fraud, deceit and oppression'; it 'would never be a good world so long as there was a lord in England'. Their words were matched by insubordinate, eccentric and sometimes violent behaviour which alarmed and frightened those whose hegemony they threatened. Fifth monarchists and other millenarian sects, though small – contemporary estimates of about 4000 now seem excessive – were even more willing to resort to violence in their attempt to create an imminent kingdom of heaven on earth. Anglican royalists saw them all as mad – 'fanatics' or, later, 'enthusiasts' – but that made them more, not less, alarming. Unamenable to reason, rejecting conventions of society and government, they recalled the horrifically bloody uprising of anabaptists in Münster in Germany in 1525, which for many gentlemen was as symbolic of the consequences of religious fanaticism as Queen Mary's burnings of protestants at Smithfield had been of the consequences of popery. One Norfolk gentleman in 1659 built up a private army, he said, 'to secure himself against the quakers and anabaptists who he heard would rise, to cut their throat first, if he could'.[4]

The biggest unknown factor in the Restoration religious settlement turned out, however, to be the most powerful. The survival of the Church of England over more than a decade and a half's proscription had been remarkable. In 1640 the nation had been almost at one against Archbishop Laud's campaign to stamp out puritanism within the Church; in the years that followed, the Church's monopoly and the foundations of its power had been removed and its services banned. But throughout the war and the Interregnum the anglican liturgy was secretly (and even, at times, openly) read with great devotion at churches throughout the country.[5] Such well-attended services gave clear evidence of a continuing and positive commitment to the Church of England. But there were many traditions within the Church: did the widespread enthusiasm for it mean a 'Laudian' rejection of puritanism and calvinistic theology, or something more moderate?

There were those in the post-1660 Church of England who shared the vehemence of Laud's anti-puritanism. Some, such as Bishop Cosin of Durham, had been his friends and protégés. There is evidence, too, that arminianism – the anti-calvinistic belief in God's universal grace and the freewill of all men to obtain salvation that had been attributed to Laud by his opponents – survived in the Church of England, although often as no more than the cultivation of personal devotion and integrity that marked the Interregnum devotional writings of Jeremy Taylor and Henry Hammond. In such a guise it had lost much of its anti-calvinist edge, and indeed took on something of puritanism's tone of moral seriousness. Many more than such 'Laudians' or anti-calvinists, however, possessed a partisan hatred of presbyterians which made any compromise of the Church of England's principles in order to gratify them unthinkable. For Anglican royalists, puritans and presbyterians had been the *agents provocateurs* who had fomented Civil War, basing their arguments for resistance to Charles I on justifications for rebellion and tyrannicide which French calvinists – as well as catholics – had developed during their own religious wars. If presbyterians were horrified by the execution of Charles I and scared by religious sectarianism, they had only themselves to blame. Their religious scruples were the effects of pride, their piety was hypocrisy. 'If these tender consciences were so good as is pretended to them they should live without offence to God and man'; said one MP in parliament in 1668: 'but what villianies did these men commit when they had the power in their hands is most notorious.' Or as another said in 1673, 'a Puritan was ever a rebel; [it] began with Calvin – these dissenters made up the whole army against the king; the destruction of the Church was then aimed at'.[6]

Yet for anglicans, affection for the Church sprang from deeper causes as well. A core of intellectually committed laymen – at all levels of society – helped to retain the integrity of the Church throughout the war and the Interregnum, sheltering its clergy, arranging its services, and maintaining its morale. They revered the doctrine and constitution of the English Church and counted it part of the very fabric of English society. Pious men, like the diarist John Evelyn, or the Treasury official Sir Philip Warwick, were determined to maintain the integrity of the Church from post-Restoration compromise as well as from pre-Restoration disintegration.[7]

Only a few possessed that level of commitment, yet there persisted a large degree of affection for the old traditional rituals and rhythms of anglican royalist worship. For many more the Church of England was a symbol of past tranquillity, unity, and above all of law. Many might sympathise with some of the moderate nonconformists' scruples, and yet be convinced that a unified church was essential for political order. Without unity in religion, one MP argued, there would result 'the rise of all sorts of heresies and villainous opinions', and with them, violent religious contention.[8] The Church's ancient status as 'the Church by law established' gave it an enormous advantage over its competitors and a powerful argument against alteration to its basic structure and doctrine: any tinkering might weaken it and render it unable to resist the tides of change. In 1669 one MP recommended that any who wished to propose any change in the religious laws should 'come as a proposer of new laws did in Athens, *with ropes about their necks*'.[9] Wrapping themselves in such language, churchmen could claim that the preservation of the Church was the only key to peace and stability. But all these were negative, rather than positive, reasons for supporting the Church. Leading churchmen were aware how limited their active support really was: the laity of England may have liked the Book of Common Prayer; they may have been fearful of the consequences of religious pluralism; but they were not particularly fond of bishops, neither did they willingly give the Church their ungrudging support against its enemies. There were even some anglican royalists (the lord treasurer the Earl of Southampton was one) who thought protestant unity against catholicism more important than the purity of anglicanism.[10]

The government itself was divided and confused over its favoured solution to the religious problem. Ever since the failure of Charles II's attempt to gain possession of his throne in concert with Scottish presbyterians in 1651, the king had been committed to a restoration of the Church of England along with his own. The experience had left him with a strong distaste for presbyterianism; throughout the Interregnum the interests of Church and monarchy had been closely linked and many of the king's closest advisers had counted the re-establishment of the Church of England essential if the monarchy's future was to be assured. Nevertheless, the king and his advisers recognised in 1660 the political necessity of compromise. The apparent power of presbyterianism, and the preference of General Monck, the country's main power-broker, for a 'moderate presbyterian government' of the Church made it seem unavoidable. The Declaration of Breda, issued from the Netherlands as the Convention Parliament was meeting, committed the government to granting 'a liberty to tender consciences' at least to those groups 'which do not disturb the peace of the kingdom' until the religious problem could be settled by Act of Parliament. The document was deeply ambiguous, failing to say when and under what circumstances the government would put forward proposals for a bill. Yet this first official statement of Restoration policy was remarkably liberal. The entry into the government at the Restoration of many presbyterian grandees – Monck, the Earl of Manchester and Lord Robartes, among several others – was another sign that royal religious policy might be diluted.

Uncertainty about the king's own religious beliefs added to the ambiguities of the Restoration settlement. Contemporaries noticed Charles's lack of interest in the formal business of religion. His tendency to fidget in religious services and his loose morality were remarked on censoriously by churchmen; his tendency to freethinking they found more alarming still. He possessed no strong sense of the constitutional and legal position of the English Church. He tolerated even quakers, regarding their unconventionality as more amusing than threatening. It was his family's penchant for Roman Catholicism, though, that was the most disturbing. Both Charles and James were strongly attracted to catholicism, the religion of their mother, Queen Henrietta Maria. As Halifax argued later, part of its attraction to Charles may have lain in its splendour in contrast with the poverty of the Church of England in exile: 'the outward appearance of such unfashionable men was made an argument against their religion; and a young prince more susceptible to raillery, was the more susceptible of a contempt for it'. It may, too, have seemed that its ritual and ceremonial could lend a more awesome atmosphere to kingship than could anglicanism: 'no other creed matches so well with the absolute dignity of kings', he told the French ambassador in 1663.[11] The rumours of Charles II's formal conversion in 1659 are unlikely to have been true, however – Charles never practised catholicism. But his favour to the small English catholic community long aroused the suspicion of English politicians; and his acceptance of absolution from a Roman Catholic priest on his deathbed indicated a final acknowledgement of his real religious allegiance. The king's sympathy for catholics gave him an attitude towards religious persecution and protestant uniformity that to churchmen was disquietingly ambivalent. It was far from certain that in its attempt to rebuild its religious monopoly the Church of England had the full support of its formal head.

The religious settlement was perhaps the most complex of all the problems that faced the government at the Restoration. There was virtually no solution which would not deeply alienate some politically influential segment of the population. Even at court there were enough different attitudes towards the question to provoke intense disagreement. In 1660, the situation was extremely volatile. The old army, still marked by religious radicalism, looked on as the numerous presbyterians in the Convention Parliament pressed for an early settlement and the anglican royalists in the restored government tried to defer a decision to a future (and hopefully more anglican) parliament. The government had to concede a provisional settlement, the Worcester House Declaration of 25 October, in which considerable concessions were made to moderate presbyterians on the role of bishops and on the revision of the Book of Common Prayer; a general synod of the Church would be called, as well, to discuss the points of difference. This was far in excess of anything previously offered to presbyterians. They won another concession, too, with the passage of a bill confirming many of the ministers who had entered into livings during the Interregnum without proper episcopal ordination. Even so, the Worcester House Declaration was merely temporary; and in any case, by the end of 1660 the Church was once again a basically anglican one: cathedral chapters had been revived; the Prayer Book was being used all over the country; and from the end of August bishops were being appointed to all the sees of England and Wales.

With the disbandment of the army and the dissolution of the Convention Parliament, some of the pressure for concessions disappeared. The elections held in March 1661 marked the political revival of the Church after its ecclesiastical resurgence: overwhelmingly royalist, the new parliament possessed a core of loyal and determined anglicans; many of the rest were sufficiently disturbed by fears of the violence of dissenters to accept their arguments. In response, the government's strategy became clearer. Still uncertain about the strength of presbyterianism in the country at large, it, or more particularly Clarendon, remained anxious to keep moderate presbyterians within the Church, perhaps by allowing ministers in their own services to omit a few offending passages from the liturgy and ceremonies, or by finding some formula to permit those who had not received episcopal ordination in the Interregnum to go on ministering to their congregations: but such concessions would be temporary, and very limited. The presbyterians were to be assimilated peacefully within the Church, and the schism between puritan and conformist in the English Church would finally be healed.

For some, however, even this was going too far. Within parliament, anglican royalists defended the integrity of the

Church against any such concession. Appealing to royalist and conservative concern over the revolutionary implications of presbyterianism, they succeeded in making the new Act of Uniformity, designed to replace the old Act of 1559, as restrictive as possible. The new Act set the doctrinal and liturgical character of the Restoration Church. It required all clergy, by 24 August 1662, to declare their 'unfeigned assent and consent' to everything in the Book of Common Prayer, and to use it in their services, to renounce the Solemn League and Covenant (the foundation document of English pres- byterianism), to be ordained according to the rite of the English Church and to subscribe fully to all of its doctrinal articles. Although the Book of Common Prayer was reviewed by a committee of divines of both persuasions, as had been envisaged in the Worcester House Declaration, any changes of substance were resisted by the bishops. The Act of Uniformity passed into law without the government achieving any of its planned concessions to presbyterians. In the summer of 1662 Clarendon tried to use the prerogative to suspend or limit the operation of the Act, but the most politically active of the bishops, Sheldon of London (soon to become Archbishop of Canterbury) argued forcibly against it, and was supported by the anglican royalists in the Privy Council: the attempt had to be dropped, leaving presbyterian ministers in their hundreds to be removed from their livings all over the country.

Presbyterians had been as concerned by the rise of the radical sects as had anglicans, and they had concurred with – even encouraged – measures aimed at them: the Act of 1661 to prevent quaker meetings was passed with their full support. But within a few years the sort of restrictions they had found acceptable against quakers were being aimed at themselves as well. In 1664, the Conventicle Act banned all groups of people meeting for religious worship outside authorised services, with penalties ranging from fines to transportation. In 1665 the 'Five Mile Act' imposed on those who had been ejected from their livings by the Act of Uniformity an obligation to accept an oath forswearing any attempt to change the constitution of the Church or the State. It completed a body of legislation that was to become known as the 'Clarendon Code'.

The title is ironic, for Clarendon had at least tried to avoid the permanent alienation of moderate presbyterians from the Church that the 'Code' had achieved. Yet in another sense it was fair. It was Clarendon and his associates who had unleashed the political power of anglicanism, by placing the dedicated anglican royalists whom they knew and trusted in the second-rank but crucial executive positions of government. From there, they wielded considerable power, nowhere more than in parliament. Devoted anglicans such as Henry Coventry, Sir Heneage Finch, Sir Job Charlton, Sir John Berkenhead and Sir Philip Warwick became the workhorses of administration and of the government's parliamentary business. As a result, the government could never effectively present its case when it backed away from uncompromising anglicanism. The mass of the Commons, the largely country gentry of the backbenches, may not have shared the deep commitment of these men to the Church. Their attitudes to presbyterianism were rarely so single-minded: the very close votes on several points in the Act of Uniformity show that many gentry were uncertain about the virtues of rejecting all compromise with presbyterians. But anglican royalists possessed powerful arguments to sway them. They played on their sense of insecurity, arguing that religious diversity was a recipe for political unrest, and that those who so urgently demanded freedom of conscience had other, political, objects closer to their hearts.[12]

Within a few years, the political power and religious influence of presbyterianism, which had seemed so considerable at the Restoration, had been decisively routed. In Scotland, where presbyterianism had been so much more strongly entrenched, its overthrow was even more striking. By September 1661 the government had resolved that episcopacy would be re-established, despite the desperate efforts of the presbyterian leaders to prevent it; legislation of 1662 forced the ejection of ministers who refused to accept the transformed situation. But while the imposition of bishops in Scotland did not mean the imposition of the anglican liturgy or a profound change in the organisation of the Church, it was bitterly resisted and politically divisive; in the years to come resistance to it and the government's response were both to become increasingly violent. By 1666 nonconformist 'covenanters' had been provoked to open rebellion. Their uprising was crushed within a month; but while it lasted it had shown up the fragility of anglican dominance in Scotland.

Even in England, anglican political dominance was surprisingly shaky, nowhere more so than at court, and churchmen, lay and clerical, had to fight hard and long over the next quarter-century to defend it and the integrity of the Church of England. In early 1663 the government introduced a bill into parliament which not only promised a relaxation of the rules of uniformity which would bring presbyterians back into the Church, but would also permit the sects freedom of worship outside it. It revealed both the split of opinion within the court – for Clarendon was horrified by it – and the willingness of some in government to contemplate a very wide toleration indeed. Among them were catholics, who sought to link toleration for those of their own religion with that of the sects. It showed anglican royalists that it was not merely the presbyterians who threatened their own predominance at court. Unsurprisingly, the bill fared in parliament no better than Clarendon's efforts on behalf of the presbyterians, and the impulse behind it was lost when its instigator, the catholic Earl of Bristol, left the court in disgrace after the failure of his accusation of treason against the lord chancellor. The sects themselves were discredited when a few of them tried, unsuccessfully, to mount a rebellion in Yorkshire late the same year.

At the end of the 1660s and in the early 1670s, however, there were fresh moves to lift the restrictions on dissenters. In mid-1667, with the government desperately in search of support as it tried to wriggle out of the financial and political crisis in which defeat in the Second Dutch War had placed it, Clarendon may again have sought contacts with presbyterians, and a bill was prepared (but never presented) in the following session of parliament intended to 'comprehend' moderate dissenters inside the Church of England, in the way that

Clarendon had envisaged in the early 1660s. Clarendon's dismissal in the summer ended this sort of approach to the religious question – at least taken on its own. Further attempts to pass a bill for 'comprehension' were either coupled with a measure for a more general toleration or intended (like Bishop Morley's of 1674) to prevent some wider indulgence from taking effect.[13]

Clarendon's removal, indeed, allowed a wider range of religious policies to flourish. The rise to tenuous power of the Duke of Buckingham, the erratic and free-thinking former royalist, and Lord Ashley, the future Earl of Shaftesbury, gave new weight to proposals for a toleration of all dissenters. Both Ashley and Buckingham were identified with the *politiques* of the 1650s who had argued then for a general liberty of conscience for all orthodox Christians. In 1668 Buckingham was probably the sponsor of discussions between the liberal-minded future Bishop of Chester, John Wilkins, various prominent nonconformist divines, and the erastian lord chief baron of the exchequer, Sir Matthew Hale, which resulted in bills for both toleration and comprehension being drawn up for submission by the government in parliament. Far from achieving their aims, they were not even read: Church leaders mounted a determined campaign against the policy, and encouraged their allies in the Commons to press rather for the renewal of the 1664 Conventicle Act, due to expire in 1669. For almost two years the renewal issue was intermittently debated, provoking popular unrest in London and a par-ticularly acrimonious paper war, before the king ultimately agreed to accept a new Conventicle Act in return for aid in obtaining supply – the taxation which, by then, the govern-ment desperately needed.[14]

The failure and reversal of the attempt to introduce liberty of conscience by act of parliament made its promoters consider other ways of doing it. In 1670 Charles and Louis XIV came to an agreement to declare a new war on the Dutch; in the same secret treaty, Charles set down his intention to declare himself a catholic. The discussions over the next two years with dissenters, and the Declaration of

Indulgence which resulted in 1672 were linked to the French alliance, even though those who worked hardest to bring the Indulgence about were told nothing about the king's decision to convert. In principle, the Indulgence was an extension of the comparatively feeble attempt in 1663 to link toleration of dissenters to that of catholics. However, it went much further. Dispensing with the ecclesiastical statutes by royal prerogative, laying claim to 'that supreme power in ecclesiastical matters which is not only inherent in us but hath been declared and recognised to be so by several statutes and Acts of Parliament', the Declaration announced that protestant dissenters would be allowed to worship in buildings licensed for the purpose, while catholics would be allowed to worship unmolested in their own homes only.

The Indulgence placed many dissenters, especially the more moderate presbyterians, in a double dilemma. First, the fact that the proposal was only for toleration, and included no proposal for relaxing the laws touching the Church of England itself, meant that if they accepted the Indulgence, presbyterians would be tacitly dropping their aspirations to be members of a unified national Church. Secondly, to take advantage of the Indulgence would be to acknowledge its lawfulness, which was a matter of considerable dispute. The king's claim to so wide a prerogative in ecclesiastical affairs which allowed him to dispense with so many of the statutes regulating the Church, was based on the original Act of Supremacy, divorcing the English Church from Rome, which transferred to the king the Pope's large powers. The whole area, however, suffered from a complete lack of definition. Even if the king did in theory possess such a supremacy, it had almost always been exercised only through parliamentary legislation; anglican royalists argued vigorously that the supremacy belonged not to the king alone, but to the king in parliament.[15]

Despite the doubts of dissenters, many accepted the Indulgence – about 1500 ministers, from many different groups, took out licences – and it did, though temporarily, revolutionise patterns of religion and local power throughout the country. But its success was largely achieved by avoiding a meeting of parliament in the year of its publication, restraining anglican political pressure against it. By 1673, however, the demands of war with the Dutch made a new session of parliament essential to vote more money: as soon as it sat there was a torrent of complaints against the Indulgence, this time strengthened by outrage at the toleration of catholic worship and what MPs regarded as a dangerous widening of the royal dispensing power. The government was forced to withdraw it. A bill was, though, offered to replace it, at least for protestant dissenters: it was clear that anglican royalists no longer had such a strong hold over MPs increasingly concerned by the threat of popery, despite their doubts about the Indulgence. Churchmen were alarmed by this trend: Sir John Duncombe warned again that 'all our properties are concerned in [the question of toleration], as well as our Religion – It [freedom of worship] is their birthright – but they ought to be bound by your laws . . . – Remember what the constitution of the kingdom is – He fears its ruin'; and early in 1674 Bishop Morley of Winchester introduced proposals for comprehension in the hope of stifling those for the wider liberty. Neither bill was passed, but the debates did indicate the beginning of a change in the anglican tone of parliament.[16]

The government, however, was moving the other way. In the aftermath of the War of 1672–4, as MPs grew more deeply suspicious of popery at court, the king tried to regain the trust and loyalty of the anglican royalists. Ministers who had been associated with the Indulgence – including Lord Ashley, now the Earl of Shaftesbury – were replaced by others, more strongly committed to the Church. Most notable amongst them was the Earl of Danby; Sir Heneage Finch, formerly solicitor general, was made lord keeper and Earl of Nottingham, and both he and the two secretaries, Joseph Williamson and Henry Coventry, were men with strong anglican connexions. Danby's aim was described by one of his admiring relations as 'to settle the Church and State; to defend the one against schismatics and papists and the other against commonwealthsmen and rebels'.[17] It was probably the most anglican government of the whole reign; few of the former presbyterians who had tempered the ministry's anglicanism in the 1660s now remained. In 1675, after consultation with the bishops, the council ordered the firm enforcement of the laws against dissent; it made elaborate plans to stimulate anglican piety by erecting a memorial to Charles I in Westminster Abbey; and most notably, it proposed a bill to limit office and the right to sit in parliament to those in communion with the Church of England. The measure dominated the politics of the session of late spring 1675, was desperately opposed by a combination of dissenters, their sympathisers, catholics, 'country' peers and the ministers whom Danby and his allies had replaced, and eventually disappeared in a deliberately engineered dispute between the two Houses. Danby was forced to keep parliament prorogued for fifteen months in order to restore his control of it; when it met again, in 1677, his bill was not reintroduced.

Danby's proposal also set off intense activity outside parliament, in London and in the press especially. The alliance of anti-episcopalian and 'country' interests in response to Danby's combination of repressive anglicanism, corruption of the Commons and (as was claimed) intriguing with the French, produced enormous pressure for the removal both of him and his parliament. It also encouraged an outpouring of anti-clerical and anti-anglican propaganda. In such works as Shaftesbury's *A Letter from a person of quality to his friend in the Country* of 1675 the Church was pilloried as the agent of Danby's despotism, and even as a stooge in a grand plan to introduce popery – a 'pimp' to the whore of Babylon, as one of the most vicious satires put it.[18] The violence of the reaction, and the success of the polemic linking Danby and the Church with catholic conspiracy, suggested that Danby's attempt to stimulate anglican royalist enthusiasm for the regime had been mistimed and misconceived. It came at a time when arguments based on the lawlessness and danger of dissent were coming to seem less compelling, for moderates on both sides were now as concerned about the possibility of popish, as of protestant, subversion.

Scotland, too, had seen a renewal of repression in the mid–1670s. The rebellion of 1666 had sent the Scottish government lurching back towards a policy of greater toleration: in 1669 an indulgence was published to allow nonconformists some exemption from ecclesiastical discipline, and to the horror of episcopalians, in the same year an Act was passed which would allow the king unlimited power over the Church. From 1673, however, the failure of the policy of leniency, and political pressures on the Earl of Lauderdale, encouraged a revival of a vigorous anti-nonconformist policy. From 1676 existing legislation against conventicles was put determinedly into effect, and new legislation passed to hasten the country's full submission to conformity. By 1677 the government had committed itself to a programme of military suppression of the nonconformists, the arbitrary and illegal excesses of which, conveyed to London by its opponents, added fuel to English parliamentary attacks on the violence and tyranny of the government in Church and State.

In Scotland and in England the most determined anglican royalists had had to work hard throughout the 1660s and 1670s to retain control of government religious policy, struggling to maintain the supremacy of the established Church against the indifference of some and the hostility of others. The struggle could be as intense, however, in the provinces. The reality of the Church of England's monopoly of worship depended very much on the willingness of local elites to enforce it. The penalties of the ecclesiastical courts, doled out to dissenters, were no longer very effective in enforcing attendance at Church against the determined. Only by enrolling the gentry, or a substantial part of them, as its allies could it maintain its power. Yet the enforcement of the 'Clarendon Code' and the Church's campaigns to crush nonconformity show the limits of gentry enthusiasm for persecuting anglicanism. The bulk of the gentry may have been willing to fight nonconformity when they believed that it posed an immediate threat to political stability, but to the despair of warmer anglicans, such lukewarm supporters were often reluctant to risk local unpopularity by harassing less obviously threatening presybterians or independents. As a result, persecution was sporadic and often ineffective.

Even the Church itself could not lay claim to a homogeneous orthodoxy, at least at parish level. The foundation of the Church's Restoration revival, the Act of Uniformity, was better enforced than the other religious Acts passed in the first five years of the Cavalier Parliament, largely because most of the responsibility for enforcing it lay with the Church authorities themselves. Altogether, 960 clergy were expelled from their benefices as a result of the Act, in addition to the many who had already been removed as a result of the Act of the Convention Parliament for restoring ministers ejected during the Civil War or Interregnum. But despite the removals, those who conformed included many who had retained their benefices or attended the puritan-controlled universities under the commonwealth or protectorate regimes in the 1650s. By 1663 about half of the churches and chapels in two dioceses – those of Canterbury and Winchester – were served by commonwealth conformists. Not all of these had necessarily harboured any sympathy for the regimes under which they performed their function: many had seen the importance of their ministerial office as overriding scruples about the conditions imposed by authority; some had managed to evade them. Some of the brightest of them – the 'latitudinarians' – became the ablest controversialists of the Church against the dissenters. Nevertheless, some of these commonwealth conformists, particularly in neglected rural areas, clung onto old, more puritan practices or were more willing in practice to relax the stricter rules of conformity (as Edward Fowler did in the London parish of Cripplegate in the 1680s) in the interests of protestant unity. Some ministers sympathised with, and retained close contacts with at least the moderate presbyterians.[19]

If the Church, with its religious tests and visitations, could not remove the temporisers and qualified conformists from its ranks, the gentry's anglicanism was much more suspect. There were energetic local justices of the peace or deputy lieutenants whose hatred of puritanism or love of the Church was strong enough to provoke them to campaign tirelessly within – and sometimes without – the law for the eradication of nonconformity. Some, like Sir Daniel Fleming in Cumberland or Colonel Corne in Glamorgan were happy to break up conventicles even when the law permitting them to do so had lapsed: the latter, asked by what authority he acted in rounding up worshipping dissenters, 'laid his hand upon his sword, and said that was his authority'.[20] Much local persecution depended on such men. The extent to which they received wider support from their neighbours among the gentry, and the others of lower status (the constables, churchwardens, tithingmen and militia men) on whom so much of a prosecution rested, depended on a number of factors. Many were reluctant to persecute any group, even quakers, for religious offences alone,[21] although at times of political and religious tension, when dissent seemed to take on a particularly threatening political aspect, they might be willing to take a more active role. General persecutions were rarely unleashed without some prompting from the central government – either in the form of a new Act or of an order to put the laws against dissent into force. The passage of the Quaker Act in 1662, the Conventicle Act in 1664, its replacement in 1670, proclamations of 1668 and 1669 against nonconformist preachers, the cancellation of the Declaration of Indulgence in 1673, and the instructions given in 1676 by assize judges for the enforcement of the laws against nonconformity, all produced national waves of persecution, although of varying strength and duration in different areas. Individual judges, on their assizes in the country, sometimes urged on persecution through the charges they delivered to local grand juries. The extent of persecution varied among different religious groups; the sects were far more likely to be harassed than were presbyterians. The quakers' refusal to conceal their conventicling, to escape from even half-hearted attempts at their arrest, to pay fines or to promise conformity in the future made them exasperating to deal with, but easy to gather up. Quakers and baptists were seen as far more dangerous than the other major sects, and local drives against them had considerable impact, though of a limited and temporary kind. How nonconformists behaved influenced the gentry's response. Overconfidence – 'boldness' – and the violent responses to persecution which sometimes occurred in the areas (such as Somerset) where nonconformity was strongest, could prompt some more moderate justices and deputy lieutenants to firmer action. For the most part, however, the Church and the more active persecutors despaired of the attitude of their colleagues. Edmund Bohun, an active Suffolk justice, complained in 1677 of the 'upstarts who, under the pretext of prudence and moderation in ecclesiastical affairs, are ruining both Church and state and are lamentably endeavouring to tear them in pieces, while by certain quibbles they altogether evade and permit others to evade the execution of the laws'.[22] Archbishop Sheldon himself in 1665 wrote that 'when you gentlemen and justices of the country with the lawyers shall join hands to assist us, we may hope for remedy, till then, I fear we shall have all cause to complain without help in many things'.[23]

The Church's shrill response to nonconformity was an exaggerated one, for as it itself sought to prove, dissenters formed a relatively small part of the community. The census ordered by Sheldon and executed by Bishop Compton of London was the best attempt to estimate the degree of support that nonconformity enjoyed across the country. There had been attempts before, in 1665 and 1669, to provide some such record, but that of 1676 was far more comprehensive and careful. The census presents great difficulties of interpretation: it was open to distortion through the practice of partial conformity, by which many classified as conformists may well also have been members of dissenting congregations, and there may have been other reasons for absenteeism apart from dissent – such as indifference – which the figures ignore. But they do paint a broad and recognisable enough picture of dissent across the country. In a population of 2.25 million the census found about 100,000 nonconformists: their concentration varied from about 10.5 per cent or 7.2 per cent of the population (in Canterbury and London) to 1.4 per cent and 0.8 per cent (in St Asaph and Bangor). As was intended, the census showed dissent as barely significant except in one or two areas. Yet it failed to show, and there is no way of telling, how few in number were those who were truly committed to maintaining the dominance of the Church of England.[24]

In fact, whatever its public confidence in its dominance, the Church was deeply concerned about the volume and quality of its support. Quite apart from the extent to which the gentry were willing to share in the work of suppressing dissent, the clergy worried about the general contempt and unpopularity in which they were held, even by many conformists. Clerical pamphleteers such as (possibly) Thomas Ken, in the 1663 *Ichabod or the five groans of the Church,* or John Eachard in *The grounds and occasions of the contempt of the clergy and religion enquired into* of 1670 attacked the hierarchy of the Church for its failure to reform its finances and the quality of its clergy. The success of dissenting critiques, such as Marvell's *Mr Smirke, or the divine in mode* or his *The Rehearsal transpros'd,* showed that there was a large and receptive audience for ridicule of the Church's pomposities and condemnation of its inadequacies. Few of the complaints – of pluralism, simony, non-residence, and indiscriminate ordination – were new: similar charges had been hurled at the Church for a century or so. Some were undoubtedly inspired by the Church's enemies. For all that, some of them were painfully true. The hierarchy was not unaware or careless of such problems: both Sheldon and his successor, Sancroft, were deeply interested in the reform of ecclesiastical ministration and administration. Yet the hold that the gentry had over the Church – their ownership of the advowsons or impropriated tithes – presented enormous obstacles to the improvement of clerical income that was at the root of many of its problems. By 1688 still almost nothing had been achieved.[25]

Yet the Church had deeper preoccupations than ecclesiastical politics and administration. Reflecting on the rebellion and regicide, as well as on their own troubles, the clergy of the Church of England concluded that these tribulations and ghastly crimes were the effects of God's displeasure at a nation, once his favourite, that had gone rotten with sin. The

Restoration was a respite from punishment: if it were to avoid its recurrence the country needed desperately to amend its ways. The Church demanded the moral regeneration of its people.

> If any nation under heaven were the Israel of God, his chosen people, we of England have been the people; and who knows, how soon our provocations will precipitate our ruin? How near our destruction may be? and how soon an offended God may un-Church us, un-people us, and for our casual and spiritual wantonness take away his gospel, and our peace from us; and let it out to others that may bring forth the fruits of it.[26]

Anglicanism became deeply moralistic and pietistic in tone, especially in the best-selling manuals by (perhaps) Richard Allestree (*The whole duty of man*), Jeremy Taylor (*Holy living and holy dying*) and Henry Hammond (*Practical catechism*). In the process, a new generation of establishment divines largely abandoned the old predestinarian theology, sloughing off old, limiting doctrines of puritanism, and demanding not a dramatic experience of 'conversion', but 'holy living', a moral and worthy life.[27]

The deepest concern of all was at the spread of atheism. 'Atheism' covered for anglicans many tendencies. Socinianism (the application of reason to the scriptures and the denial of the divinity of Christ, and even of the Trinity) and 'Hobbism' (an argument that what were claimed to be religious laws were in reality no more than the inventions of men) were still the province of cranks and intellectuals – the scientific *virtuosi* of the Royal Society in particular – and the occasional aristocratic free-thinker, such as John Wilmot, Earl of Roches-ter, or the Duke of Buckingham. Rather more common were cynicism about and indifference towards established religion. Churchmen worried about the spread of atheism as much as about the power of dissent: declining affection for the Church threatened both its power and influence and (even more) its mission.[28]

In the 1670s and 1680s, however, the Church rediscovered its other enemy. For seventeenth-century Englishmen, the fear of popery had an almost unique power to turn political argument into violence. It was both a symptom of their insecurity and a partial cause of it. Brought up on a diet of Foxe's *Acts and Monuments*, on stories of popish massacres of protestants in the 1550s and (in Paris) in 1572, of the Gunpowder Plot of 1605 and deliverance from the Spanish Armada in 1588, they were taught to believe in an international catholic conspiracy for the eradication of protestantism; in the ruthlessness of the jesuits, the bloody advance guard and fifth column of catholicism; and in the papists' willingness to kill and break oaths because the end – the victory of the papacy – justified the means. Most recently the massacres of protestant settlers by catholic rebels in the Irish rebellion of 1641 had produced lurid and horrific stories of the barbaric practices of the papists. Fear of popery was not just the hatred of one religious sect for another; it was fear of a force which was thought to operate outside the normal laws of civilised society. Dissenters may have been more inclined than others to subscribe to parts of the anti-catholic myth – such as to see the pope as antichrist, which lent anti-popery some of its powerful apocalyptic tone – but respectable anglican royalists, such as Sir Edward Phelips in Somerset, were just as obsessed with the violence of the catholic Counter-Reformation.[29]

That this should be so was rather extraordinary in a country in which catholicism was insignificant. Compton's 1676 census estimated that there were no more than 14,000 catholics in England and Wales, and although there is much room for doubt about the figure's accuracy – papists who disguised their real religion were difficult to identify – it did reflect the minor significance of catholic recusancy in most parts of the country.[30] Protestantism was firmly in the ascendant, and catholics were kept in check by a collection of laws which forbade the celebration of the mass – even if they were rarely enforced. But the terror of popery was not derived from the small, politically inert, native catholic population, but came mainly from beyond the Channel. Protestantism in Western Europe was, by the late seventeenth century, marginalised and in retreat, threatened on all sides by great, strong catholic states. West of the Baltic, England and the Netherlands remained its principal outposts. Spain's long war against the Dutch, and her sixteenth-century crusade against heretical England, had lent the defence of protestantism an epic quality; but since her peace with the Dutch in 1648, France had gradually taken her place as the principal oppressor of the reformed religion. France's own protestants were under increasing pressure from their government and the Church; from 1669 Louis XIV began to squeeze protestant liberties of worship and to encourage conversions; his invasion of the Netherlands in 1672 was described, by the French themselves, as a religious war. By the mid-1670s France was firmly identified as the leader of a resurgent continental catholicism, and Englishmen saw the fortunes of popery and France as intimately linked: as Sir William Coventry said in parliament in 1676 'in respect of France and popery, all other things are but trifles. Popery may be here without France, but 'tis impossible that France should be here without popery.'[31] Ireland presented a different sort of catholic threat; it was an overwhelmingly catholic country, a short sail from England, peopled (the English believed) by a wild, ungovernable race, the protestant ascendancy uneasily maintained by a small and ill-equipped army. Almost encircled by popery, England felt herself to be the next target in the counter-attack of European catholicism: the last 'bulwark of liberty, protestantism and Christian faith in general, throughout the world: the main bank, that hinders the see of Rome from over-whelming all Christian nations with an universal inundation of tyranny and superstition'.[32]

Protestantism was the proud badge of England's national identity, what marked her off from the superstitious despotisms of continental Europe; England was the elect nation, escaped from the Babylonian captivity of Rome, her trials and tribulations like those the Israelites had undergone from the barbarity and idolatry of the Egyptians. But anti-catholicism was also the ordinary Englishman's ugly, visceral response to a sense of insecurity. Catholics were the nation's scapegoats, its figures of hate, to be blamed for her divisions and political crises, to be turned against whenever things went seriously wrong. Many exiled royalists, however, possessed a rather more sophisticated outlook. To men like Clarendon, who had spent more than a decade in catholic communities abroad, the unreasoning strength of English anti-catholicism, when it showed in response to the burning of London in 1666, came as a shock.[33] To another exile, Dr Isaac Basire, who had travelled widely in Europe and the Near East, William Prynne's words to him at about the same time of 'fears and jealousies, of plots and designs of jesuits and Romanists against our Church and religion' tasted of another age.[34] Yet the fear of 1666 was real enough; it should have served as a warning to the government how nasty anti-catholic feeling was, and how easily it could be aroused. Neither Charles II nor his brother chose to learn from it.

From way before 1660, there had been pressure on Charles to improve the position of catholics in England: from his mother, Henrietta Maria; from Louis XIV, whom he respected and who impressed him (rather disingenuously) with the grandeur of a prince whose power could embrace those of all religious beliefs; and from the English catholics themselves – perhaps most of all through the Earl of Bristol, but also through Lord Arundell of Wardour, their acknowledged political leader. The support of the English catholics for the Indulgence Bill introduced into parliament in early 1663, even though it made no mention of them, made clear the intention – briefly stated in the Declaration of Indulgence which had announced the bill – to secure some greater liberty for catholics. The reaction against the bill, however, showed in part the depth of animosity towards such a project that still existed. Suspicions of the government's intentions towards catholicism were strengthened when the Earl of Bristol, in his impeachment of Clarendon in July, denounced the lord chancellor's contacts with the papal court.[35]

They were increased even more by the government's attitude to the settlement of Ireland after the Restoration. The Irish rebellion of 1641 had been put down by Cromwellian soldiers who had received, as their reward, the confiscated estates of the rebels; in confiscating estates, however, the army had been fairly indiscriminate, and the Cromwellian repression of Ireland had left the question of landownership hopelessly confused. The government's attempts after 1660 to sort it out brought accusations of its favour to the Irish, and some damaging rumours of Charles I's own part in instigating the 1641 rebellion.[36] In fact, the settlement did little to reverse the expulsion of many old catholic landowners, and between 1641 and 1688 the share of the land owned by native Irish was reduced from 59 to 22 per cent. But English protestants could not be dissuaded from their belief; when the prices fetched by English cattle fell dramatically in the mid-1660s, their owners blamed cheap Irish imports and passed a bill in parliament banning them. It was a veiled attack on what were seen as the pro-Irish and pro-catholic attitudes of the current government regime in Ireland, and exposed fears of Ireland's economic aggrandisement at England's expense. The removal of the Duke of Ormonde as lord lieutenant of Ireland in 1669 might have been seen by some as restoring protestant self-confidence; in fact, under his successors, the catholics found greater favour. Restrictions on the Catholic Church were relaxed; by 1672 many of the limits imposed on the freedom of the Irish had fallen into abeyance; by January 1673 Irish catholics were even being admitted to public office. English MPs became alarmed: Henry Powle declared in 1672 'there has been a general design to set up the Popish and Irish interest, to out the Protestant and English'.[37]

English suspicions of the influence of catholicism within both the English and Irish governments were by 1672 perfectly justified. By 1669 the Duke of York had abandoned his allegiance to the Church of England, although it was not until 1672 that he was formally received into the Roman Church. There was nothing very complicated about James, and nothing very complicated about his conversion: his decision seems to have been based on little else than a personal conviction of the authority of Rome. The motives of the king himself, in declaring at a meeting in January 1669

before James, Lord Arundell and two of his closest advisers –
the Earl of Arlington and Lord Clifford (who were themselves
to become catholics) – that he intended to convert to
catholicism and to promote catholicism in England, are far
from clear. In the following year, Charles signed a secret
treaty with Louis XIV. It contained a clause affirming his
intention to declare his conversion and a commitment by
Louis to provide £200,000 to help suppress the political
disorder that the announcement would inevitably cause.
Charles was undoubtedly attracted by catholicism; but the
fact that he never announced his 'conversion', that he
remained within the anglican communion almost until the
moment of his death, and the obvious foolhardiness of such a
project in a country that had already revealed its profound
aversion to popery, have made historians deeply sceptical of
the sincerity of his promise, fitting it instead firmly into the
context of his manoeuvres to try to snatch a French alliance
away from the Dutch in 1668–70. Even if the decision was a
genuine one, it is clear that over the following year Charles, in
a cooler assessment of his position, recognised its unwisdom.
Although the firmness of Charles's affection for the Church of
England was often doubted, and the existence of a secret
treaty generally suspected, this clause of it was never known
in his lifetime.[38]

Nevertheless, the Declaration of Indulgence which was
published at almost the same time as the declaration of war
against the Netherlands made clear the government's determination to obtain some sort of toleration for catholics. Even
if many anglican royalists were chiefly perturbed for the
present by its concessions to protestant dissenters, the implications for the rise of popery were in the long term no less
worrying. As suspicions of James's conversion – and even of
Charles's – grew throughout 1672, the influence of catholicism
within the government became a major political issue. When
parliament met in 1673 for the first time since the issue of the
Declaration, members expressed their concern through
demands for the removal of catholic officers from the army
which York commanded (despite the government's protests

that there were only sixteen) and a bill which would effectively ban all catholics (and some protestant dissenters) from public office. Despite resistance from James and others, the government, desperate for supply, felt forced to accept the bill.

The Test Act was a catalyst which finally pushed popery at court to centre stage. When both James and the lord treasurer, Lord Clifford, resigned their offices shortly before the Act came into force, the rumours were confirmed. Gilbert Burnet marked 1673 as the beginning of a new phase in Restoration politics: 'hitherto the reign of King Charles was pretty serene and calm at home. . . . But the court had now given such broad intimations of an ill design both on our religion and the civil constitution, that it was now open and barefaced.'[39] Towards the close of the session of parliament, a Dutch propagandist pamphlet, *England's appeal from the private cabal at Whitehall to the great council of the nation*, was circulating in London. Claiming that the French attack on the Netherlands was the first stage in a religious war that Louis XIV had declared against protestantism, it insinuated that English ministers, corrupted by Louis, had been furthering his plans. It was an analysis which had only been waiting to be stated: it was obvious, too, who was the most corrupted of all.

The government's attempts to still the growing alarm by banishing all catholics save James himself from court and reversing the trend towards toleration in Ireland, were completely overshadowed by James's second marriage. The Duke's first wife, Anne Hyde, had died – a catholic – in 1671. Alarmed by the possibility that parliament in its next session might prevent him from making a catholic his second wife, in the summer of 1673 he pre-empted any such moves by marrying, on Louis XIV's advice, the Italian catholic daughter of the Duchess of Modena, Mary Beatrice. The proxy marriage (Mary did not arrive in England until November), coinciding with the massing of troops near London for a projected invasion of the Netherlands, created a high degree of anti-catholic excitement. When parliament met again at the end of October there was an immediate outcry against the marriage. Both Houses voted an address requesting that it be not consummated, and under increasing pressure the government broke up, ministers either joining in the attack on the Duke, as Shaftesbury did, or trying to lay the blame for the drift to popery on their political rivals, as did Buckingham and Arlington. Parliament demanded more measures to protect the protestant religion; MPs' attacks on James were taken far further by popular satirists, who saw him as at the head of a popish plot to subvert the country's religion and with it, its liberty. 'I'll have old England know', one of them pictured him saying,

> I ne'er can fight in a more glorious cause
> Than to destroy their liberty and laws
> Their House of Commons and their House of Lords
> Their parchment precedents and dull records.[40]

Bills were proposed in the lords to secure the protestant religion: one would prevent James's marriage without approval of parliament, the penalty for the breach of which, proposed the former Cromwellian Earl of Carlisle and the royalist Viscount Halifax, should be exclusion from succession to the throne; another would force any children James might have by his new wife to be brought up as protestants. The session became more and more unruly, as a coalition of discontented peers and MPs built up around the issue of York and catholicism at court. Charles was forced to prorogue parliament.

The king's solution to the current crisis was, through Danby, to appeal to anglican royalism, while pulling out of the war against the Netherlands, and demonstrating the firmness of the government's commitment to protestantism. In late 1673 and 1674 the government stimulated a wave of convictions for popish recusancy. Danby tried to reduce the terror of the Duke of York's catholicism by introducing bills in 1677 to bring his children up as protestants, to prevent a catholic king from exercising royal authority in the Church – placing it instead in the hands of the bishops – and to introduce a limited, but strictly regulated, toleration for catholics. None of these proved acceptable: MPs objected to their inadequacy, and anti-prelatists attacked the power Danby would give to the bishops.

Danby did succeed for a time in making York less of a political issue – if only by accidentally diverting popular (and particularly dissenting) hatred onto himself. But the importance of popery as an issue had not diminished. Danby's own attitudes and policies were labelled 'popish' and arbitrary by those who saw in them the same degree of religious compulsion, indifference to private conscience, and obsession with domination as they claimed to see in catholicism. By 1677 they had produced a lively 'country' opposition, particularly of presbyterians and other dissenters and their sympathisers, and a deeply entrenched suspicion of the government's inclination to a change of religion as well as of government.[41]

At the end of 1677, Andrew Marvell's famous pamphlet, *An account of the growth of popery and arbitrary government in England*, issued a clarion call for the defence of England against Rome:

> there is no Englishman that hath a soul, a body or an estate to save, that loves either God, his king, or his country, but is by all these tenures bound, to the best of his power and knowledge, to maintain the established protestant religion.[42]

By 1678, England's deep sense of insecurity had almost swivelled, once more, from fear of radical protestantism to fear of predatory catholicism. The burst of paranoia that followed when, late that year, the undefined belief in a popish conspiracy seemed to be confirmed was almost to blow England apart.

4

CONFLICTS ABROAD

The uncertainty and insecurity which dominated England's domestic politics appeared equally to guide her involvements abroad. The abiding image of England's external relations during the Restoration is one of weakness and appeasement: the whigs condemned Charles II for 'the delivery . . . of the people into the subjection of a foreign power'; James II, wrapped up in his plans at home, ignored Europe almost entirely until it took an unwelcome interest in him.[1] Historians since the seventeenth century have censured their humiliating subservience to France. Certainly, political troubles at home strongly influenced their conduct abroad, and Charles II's willingness to sacrifice English interests in pursuit of the French alliance was often extraordinary. But in fact, Charles's foreign policy was (particularly at the beginning of his reign) if anything overambitious, a cause of weakness, rather than its effect. Some of the feebleness of English policy reflected not weakness but uncertainty about England's real interests in a Europe undergoing considerable political change – a question on which her king and her people would eventually develop diametrically opposed views. And England's interests abroad extended well beyond Northern Europe: the Restoration saw a rapid expansion of England's involvement overseas; intense competition with the French and Dutch for European, American, Asian and African commerce; and a tentative approach towards a new relationship with her haphazardly founded (and haphazardly governed) colonies.

The view that the Commonwealth and Protectorate had taken of England's interests had veered between a ruthless defence of her trade and the sentimental promotion of a European protestant alliance. In 1652 the republic declared war on the Dutch because of a series of commercial disputes; two years later Cromwell ended the war and tried to negotiate a union of the two countries. A year later, he began a war with Spain, impelled not only by the radical protestant's dislike of the catholic Leviathan, but also by a desire to capture some of the Spanish trade in the West Indies. Cromwell's conduct of foreign policy may have been amateurish, but the power he could wield was astonishing. England's navy and her professional and disciplined army were new and impressive weapons in international relations; her victories against the Dutch and the Spanish startled Europe and swelled English pride. Edmund Waller expressed that power and pride in his praise of Cromwell:

> The sea's our own; and now all nations greet,
> With bending sails, each vessel of our fleet;
> Your power extends as far as winds can blow
> Or swelling sails upon the globe may go.[2]

After years of diplomatic impotence England now possessed an instrument of international influence. In 1660 it fell suddenly into the monarchy's hands. How, speculated the rulers of the neighbouring states, would the new regime use it?

The year 1660 marked a caesura not only in English affairs but also in those of the continent. Spanish economic and political decline and French revival had been signalled a year earlier in the treaty which ended their long war. One of its terms, Louis XIV's marriage to the infanta of Spain, might even lead to the Spanish empire's absorption by France, should the sickly male heir of King Philip IV not survive him. Two years later, the young Louis assumed personal control of his own kingdom at the death of Cardinal Mazarin, and began a relentless search for glory. In 1658 a new emperor, Leopold I, was elected in the Hapsburg empire, and there was change in the North, too, as the death of the aggressive King Charles X of Sweden and the succession of a minor brought to an end a period of war and expansion. The United Provinces of the Netherlands had since 1648 been at peace with their old enemy, Spain, and were developing increasingly close diplomatic and commercial ties with her; inevitably the *rapprochement* raised the question of the future of the traditional Dutch–French alliance. Did Dutch security now best lay in friendship with France, or in keeping both of the European superpowers at arm's length?

England confused them all. The events of 1660 were as great a surprise on the continent as they were at home. No country had been certain enough of the prospects of a Stuart Restoration to offer Charles II unstinting help: the exiled court had been excluded from France in 1655; and although Spain formally offered Charles a pension and discussed military aid, her assistance was ill-paid and her interest desultory. The Dutch republic had been even less enthusiastic: the marriage of Charles's sister to the 'stadhouder' of most of its constituent Provinces, Prince William II of Orange, with whom the republic's states-general struggled for power, had firmly identified the English monarchy with the anti-republican faction in Dutch politics. After William's death in 1650, Charles was to disagree with the states-general over the guardianship of William's infant son, also William. When England and the Netherlands agreed to peace in 1654, the states of Holland, the most powerful of the seven Provinces, had accepted the English government's demands for a permanent exclusion of the Orange family from its stadhoudership. With the growth in power of Johan De Witt, the pensionary of the Province of Holland and the most powerful figure in the federation, the anti-orangists were firmly in control.

Spain had the strongest claim to the restored monarchy's friendship. After the Restoration, Philip IV poured diplomatic effort into England, offering a formal end to Cromwell's war and hoping for help against Portugal (with which he had been waging a bitter war since its secession in 1640) and the restoration of Dunkirk and Jamaica, Cromwell's prizes from the war. Portugal, however, also had an alliance to offer, backed by France: Louis XIV was happy to see Spain's difficulties continue, despite the 1659 treaty which barred him from active involvement in them. Otherwise, France was curiously casual about her relations with England; Louis XIV, preoccupied with the strengthening of France's eastern borders, and with the encouragement of French commercial power, was more anxious to renew the old alliance with the Dutch than to conclude a new one with England. The Dutch themselves picked their way cautiously through a diplomatic minefield. Tentatively, they offered France and England a triple alliance in the hope of keeping the army of the one and the navy of the other at arm's length.

Which alliance to choose? Commercial interests, politicians and courtiers, and popular pressure all pushed the English government in various directions. But the greatest influence on the making of English foreign policy was the king himself. Idle and inattentive he may have been in domestic politics, but this was never the case in foreign affairs. It was clear (as it was not always in some other spheres) that Charles was fully in charge. Rather than defensive and negative, his instincts seemed to some of those who saw him early in his reign to be aggressive, even belligerent. The French ambassador, D'Estrades, noticed his 'great ambition and desire to make war'.[3] In the principal choice, between alignment with France or Spain, Charles naturally preferred France. Not that he was hostile to Spain: he had been on good terms with Philip IV's principal minister and knew that Spain had rich prizes if she cared to offer them – above all a share of her trade in the Americas and West Indies. Yet Charles felt closer to France; an alliance with the rising and dynamic Louis XIV seemed to hold out prospects of power and glory far greater than those that could be had in conjunction with a country so severely set in economic and political crisis as was Spain. Most of all, though, the English government sought French friendship to pre-empt what the Protectorate, before it, had feared: a Franco-Dutch alliance to partition the Spanish Netherlands and take command of the Channel, leaving England's security and her trade at the mercy of her commercial rivals.[4] Besides this, the Restoration monarchy retained an ineradicable suspicion of the republican Netherlands, a haven since early in the century for England's refugee radicals. For political as well as commercial reasons, the English government was never happy while the United Provinces were strong and stable.[5]

Yet whatever her purely political and strategic interests, England's trade dominated her foreign policy. Following the example of the Rump Parliament, the government had established soon after the Restoration an advisory council of trade whose members included politicians and merchants, with which the king and council might consult on commercial issues.[6] The government drew heavily on economic and commercial advice from others as well, in particular Sir George Downing, who served both the Protectorate and the Restoration regimes as envoy to the United Provinces.[7] If for no other reason, merchants possessed considerable influence over the government through their hold over its finances: the great merchants included the Crown's biggest lenders. England's policy may not have been 'mercantilist' – built around the encouragement of the expansion of the nation's exports – yet it is clear that the English government recognised the importance of trade for the country's power.

English trade was still heavily weighted towards the Mediterranean, and particularly towards Spain (see table). In

Destinations of domestic exports from and sources of imports to London, average of 1663 and 1669 (percentages)

	Ireland/ Scotland	NW Europe	Baltic, Scandinavia Russia	Spain, Portugal Mediterranean	Far East	America
EXPORTS						
Woollens	0.4	31.7	5.5	56.5	1.3	4.6
All goods	1.8	36.6	4.4	47.8	1.4	8.0
IMPORTS						
All goods	0.8	36.7	7.8	31.0	11.7	12.0

Source: C.G.A. Clay *Economic Expansion and Social Change: England 1500–1700* (2 vols, Cambridge, 1984), II, *Industry, Trade and Government*, pp. 142 and 160, tables xi and xx.

the 1660s, almost 48 per cent of London's exports went to Spain, Portugal and the Mediterranean. Spanish wool and Spanish markets were essential to the English clothing industry; the Mediterranean carrying trade was one area in which English shipping still had the edge over the Dutch. The conclusion – the importance of peace in the Mediterranean and good relations with Spain – was backed up by the damage that Cromwell's war had done to English commerce. Yet other conclusions were possible. The reluctance of the Spanish to open their colonial trade to the English was a point of immense irritation: the war of 1655 had at least partly been designed to attempt its opening by force. An alliance with Portugal might bring new privileges in the large Portuguese empire in South America, South-West Africa, India and the Far East.

England's merchants, however, had to conduct their business in the face of vigorous competition, particularly from the Dutch, but increasingly from the French as well. Dutch merchants were their rivals for the continental carrying trade, for the fisheries of the North Sea, for trade in Africa, the East Indies and the Baltic and for the position of major European *entrepôt*. Merchants bitterly complained at what they saw as the aggressiveness of the Dutch; politicians feared England's decline into a commercial satellite of the Netherlands. That fear made them aggressive as well; in a belief that the amount of trade was finite, and there was not enough for both countries, some of the English resolved to push the Dutch out of it before they were pushed out themselves. 'The Truth is', wrote Lord Holles, 'they would have all that trade, and will try a bloody nose before they quit their pretensions.'[8] French merchants rivalled the English in exports to the Levant, trade with Spain and the Spanish empire, the Newfoundland fisheries and the North American fur trade. During the 1660s Louis XIV's *contrôleur-général*, Colbert, attempted to renovate French trade and industry, protecting it in the meantime with discriminatory duties on imports: by 1667 the French customs tariff on English cloth had been raised to almost nine times its 1644 level. At home, politicians became aware of England's

large trade deficit with France; luxury goods, particularly
wines and linens, were blamed for what Samuel Fortrey, in
England's interest and improvement, calculated in 1663 as an
annual deficit of £1.6 million.

Popular political preferences and prejudices tended to reflect
the pro-Spanish, anti-Dutch and anti-French attitudes of the
majority of the English mercantile community. The Dutch, for
sure, were still viewed in many quarters as isolated and heroic
protestant pioneers in a popish wilderness; yet pro-Dutch
feeling was often politically motivated, most powerful among
republicans and protestant romantics, such as Algernon
Sidney or Slingsby Bethel. Bethel vigorously defended them in
his 1671 *The present interest of England stated*:

> in the generality of their morals [the Dutch] are a reproach to
> some nations . . . I cannot think their trade or wealth (although I
> believe that Holland singly taken is the richest spot of ground . . .
> since the creation) to be a good or honest foundation for a
> quarrel; for their commerce [is] alone the effect of industry, and
> ingenuity.[9]

But even when they felt their religious cousinhood with the
Dutch, the generality of England could not regard them with
affection, and saw them only through the eyes of commercial
rivals. They held them in contempt for their bourgeois
preoccupation with profit, and in envy for their commercial
success.[10]

It was for the French, however, that Englishmen reserved
their deepest contempt, which was mingled, by the end of the
1660s, with a touch of fear. English popular opinion was
already in the early 1660s more favourable to Spain than it
was to France, despite, or perhaps because of, Cromwell's
war. The war had in any case encouraged a recognition of the
vital part the Spanish trade played in England's economy.
France's perfidy in concluding a separate peace with Spain in
1659, and her efforts to squeeze England's trade in the late
1650s and early 1660s stimulated English resentment. When
the entourages of the French and Spanish ambassadors in
London clashed over precedence in 1661, the Spanish 'victory'

was greeted in London with pleasure: 'indeed', wrote Pepys, 'we do naturally all love the Spanish and hate the French'.[11] If unedifying in many other ways, the incident and its sequel served as a warning of Louis XIV's determination to assert French pre-eminence all over Europe. Already in the mid-1660s some European statesmen were worried by his ambition: in 1664 an English diplomat, Sir William Temple, called him 'this great comet that is risen of late . . . who expects not only to be gazed at but adored by all the world'.[12] Within a few more years, the assessment was common to everywhere in Europe.

England's own title to respect and influence throughout Europe in the 1650s was derived from the powerful army and navy that had been built up by parliament and the Common-wealth. But by the end of the disbandments of 1660–1 Charles II's army was minute in comparison with Louis XIV's. The navy remained largely intact; with 156 ships, half of them major fighting ships-of-the-line, it was a force which (though in poor repair) could stand comparison with the major continental navies.[13] The Restoration government could scar-cely afford it. However impressive the navy might be, using it as more than an occasional adjunct of diplomacy was cripplingly expensive.[14] Interregnum governments had paid for their aggressive foreign policy by heavy and punitive taxation and the sale of assets; even then they had found it impossible to maintain all of the navy's commitments. The Restoration government, with fewer resources at its disposal, attempted to do many of the things that its predecessors had done. Not surprisingly it found itself ruined by the expense. England was not unique in this: the wars waged by France in 1635–59 and 1688–1714 were paid for by the sale of offices, loans at high rates of interest, and often by reneging on government debt. The Dutch were capable of withstanding such pressures because of their more sophisticated system of public credit; even so, war could put a dangerous strain on the govern-ment's finances. England's system of parliamentary taxation, however, made her particularly vulnerable. Foreign ambas-sadors recognised this weakness and increasingly tried to exploit parliamentary politics in an effort to obstruct or to encourage involvement in European conflicts.

Right at the beginning of the reign, Spain's ambassador had clumsily tried such intrigues. The Spanish had been quick to open negotiations with the restored monarchy: a truce was agreed to halt the current war, and negotiations began on a firmer treaty. Yet the Spanish had little sense of the weakness of their position. They peremptorily demanded that Jamaica and Dunkirk be restored, and that England declare war on Portugal; they refused to allow English trade or expansion in the Americas. Deeply dissatisfied, the English government listened to Portugal, while the Spanish ambassador raged and tried ineffectively to agitate in parliament. Portugal, desperate for help, offered far more: her king's sister in marriage; a large cash dowry (more, in truth, than the country could afford); substantial trading privileges in Portugal and her empire; and the cession of Tangier in North Africa and Bombay in India. In return, she requested troops. The blessing of France and her promise to pay much of the cost of the soldiers clinched the treaty. In June, the alliance was signed, committing England to defend Portuguese independence. Inevitably, the Portuguese were soon in difficulties over the payment of the dowry and the English troops, and Spain's reaction to the treaty threatened to drag England back into war. Spanish relations with England froze, particularly with the arrival of the Infanta Catherine in England and her marriage to Charles II in May 1662, and the despatch of about 4000 troops to Portugal in the same month. Soon afterwards, the English force took part in the defeat of a Spanish offensive in Portugal, and English privateers attacked Cuba the same year. The Spanish, in response, tried to stimulate unrest in England and Ireland and strengthened their alliance with the Dutch, granting them what they had refused England – new and sweeping trading privileges in their empire.[15]

England's falling-out with Spain made a French alliance particularly desirable. Steps had already been taken to obtain one. The marriage, in August 1660, of the king's sister Henriette-Anne to Louis XIV's brother, the Duke of Orleans, had confirmed the close links between the two royal families, and the death of the architect of the Cromwellian alliance of 1654, Cardinal Mazarin, in 1661, removed an obstacle to better relations. Negotiations began on a close personal treaty with Louis XIV. In the midst of them, in 1662, as a mixture of economy measure and token of goodwill, the English government sold Dunkirk to France for £340,000. Englishmen saw the sale as demeaning, and although it worsened relations with Spain still further, it had little effect on Louis XIV's attitude towards England. Charles had hoped, above all, to pre-empt any renewal of the Franco-Dutch alliance. But in their negotiations, the French always placed their relations with the Netherlands above those with England, and the Dutch were thankful for their interest, anticipating that it might not be long before their commerce was again threatened by English force. In April 1662 they renewed and strengthened their old defensive alliance with France: the treaty included a clause, obviously aimed at England, guaranteeing the freedom of navigation, commerce and fishing.

The 1662 treaty marked the beginning of a decline in Anglo-French relations. It did little to improve Anglo-Dutch relations either. Negotiations on a whole range of disputes that bedevilled England's relations with the Netherlands began in November 1660 in a fairly moderate atmosphere. The disputes over the position of Prince William of Orange were quickly settled, with the Dutch agreeing to revoke his exclusion from the stadhoudership of Holland. Thereafter, however, the negotiations became progressively less cordial. The Dutch were disappointed by the renewal of the English restrictions on the use of foreign shipping in English and colonial trade; all the old disagreements on trade, and old tales of violence and lawlessness by the trading companies on each side were revived, and new ones added; there were violent confrontations in 1661 and 1662 between rival trading fleets in West Africa, and the negotiators were lobbied ferociously by the merchant communities on both sides. A treaty was concluded in September 1662, although it failed to settle very much: English and Dutch merchants complained bitterly about its terms and effectively ignored them. In 1663 an English expedition set out to capture West African ports, using royal ships; in August 1664 the English government ordered the occupation of the Dutch colony of the New Netherlands, in America.

Some in the English government did all they could to promote a confrontation. The Duke of York, in particular, backed the more belligerent merchant interests: he was in part behind the New Netherlands expedition and the Royal Africa Company's 1663 attack on Dutch possessions in Africa, and was, above all, eager to emulate under his own command the naval successes of the war of 1652–4.[16] Others, however, viewed with apprehension the possible effects of war on both the country's finances and religious and political unrest. Charles, in 1663 and early 1664, largely agreed with them, and favoured continued, if rather brutal, negotiation. Yet as the confrontations escalated in the course of 1664, as England's honour came to seem besmirched by the treatment meted out to her ships and merchants, and as parliament seemed to be willing to support its vindication, Charles began to succumb. When parliament was persuaded to grant the extraordinary sum of £2.5 million for the war in late 1664, he even became enthusiastic.[17]

For France, a war was deeply unwelcome. Louis XIV was carefully preparing to assert his wife's claim to part of the Spanish Crown's inheritance in the Spanish Netherlands if – as seemed likely – Philip IV's death, expected daily, should precipitate a crisis over the Spanish succession. A war in which he would be bound by treaty to help the Dutch against an aggressor could ruin his plans. He tried hard to make peace between the two parties, but in February 1665 the English, unmollified, declared war. In April the two fleets sailed; in early June they fought off the Suffolk coast. The battle was a dramatic victory for the Duke of York; but perhaps more important than the naval action to the outcome of the war was the diplomatic action, in which England found herself increasingly isolated. It became clearer during the year that Louis XIV would probably honour his treaty with the

Dutch – if for nothing else, at least to prevent England from winning a position of naval supremacy, and to secure a rapid end to the war, made urgent by Philip IV's death in September. Not that most of England minded: the possibility of France entering the war led to a surge of patriotic and Francophobe enthusiasm, and helped to persuade parliament to grant a further £1.25 million in November. In January 1666 France declared war.

France's entry into the war was in fact a serious blow to England's prospects of winning it, and made her search for allies more desperate. She at first found little sympathy in Spain; and her one ally in Germany, the Prince-Bishop of Münster, who had his own reasons for hostility to the Netherlands, was soon forced out of the war by French troops. The Emperor Leopold I, though nervous about French intentions in the Spanish Netherlands, refused to commit himself without his Spanish cousins; Spain would not enter the war until she had secured peace with Portugal; and Portugal, still winning victories and now backed unstintingly by French money, refused to negotiate. Throughout 1666 English envoys unsuccessfully tried to square this vicious diplomatic circle, hinting at a grand league against France to guarantee the Spanish Netherlands. Everywhere they found that French money had been there before them, or that threats closer to home blocked out the danger to the Spanish Netherlands.

England's naval fortunes declined, too. In July 1666, in four days of fierce fighting her fleet was almost overwhelmed by the Dutch; in the colonies she lost Surinam, on the north-east coast of South America, to the Dutch, and St Kitts, Antigua and Montserrat in the West Indies to the French. Both Dutch and English trade was badly affected by the interruption of war: England's trade had shrunk almost to nothing.[18] English hardship was increased still further by the severe epidemic of plague from the summer of 1665 and the Fire of London in September 1666. It was penury, however, that was strangling England's war effort. Repairs and supplies to naval ships, building and fitting out new ones, and the (too often neglected) payments to seamen, absorbed a huge amount of money. Enormous taxes – as heavy as any imposed in the Civil War – were granted by parliament, but England's primitive system of government borrowing prevented them from being much use. The taxes were paid over a long period: the government needed its money immediately. At the same time, the decline in trade meant a drastic drop in customs and excise receipts. The government's difficulties were multiplied when, in the parliamentary session of 1666–7, the trade and agricultural depression together with the burden of taxes, the disruption provoked by able and ambitious courtiers, and confusion and distrust within the government, combined to delay the discussion of supply until late in the session. The final grant of £1.8 million was large, but effectively useless, as most of it would not begin to be payable for over a year. At the end of February, faced with a desperate shortage of money, the government had no means of fitting out a full fleet for the season's campaigning.[19]

By then, there was at least hope that the war would soon be ended: the Dutch were as anxious for peace as were the English; and it was now overshadowed by the anticipation that Louis' attack on the Spanish Netherlands, perhaps provoking a general war in Europe, was imminent. Philip IV's death left Spain with a feeble infant king and a miserably divided regency. All Europe expected that Louis would shortly take advantage of her weakness to claim that the arcane traditions of inheritance in Flanders meant that his wife, Philip IV's daughter, was the rightful heir in the Spanish Netherlands. In the diplomatic manoeuvres of the summer of 1667, with Leopold I's ambassador, the Freiherr von Lisola, trying to put together an anti-French alliance, the end of the Anglo-Dutch war seemed a mere detail. Charles II hoped that France would bring the Dutch to accept English terms. But Louis XIV was reluctant, as ever, to lose Dutch goodwill. When, at the peace conference at Breda in May 1667, the English demanded more concessions from the Dutch than its negotiators felt that their position warranted, De Witt sent the Dutch fleet to deliver the final blow of the war against an unprepared English fleet. Sailing up the Medway to Chatham, the Dutch captured the flagship of the Royal Navy, and burnt or sank four other of its biggest vessels. The disaster provoked a political storm in London, and English diplomats at Breda hastily dropped their demands. Despite the Dutch success, the settlement was a fairly moderate one: England accepted Dutch claims in the East Indies and West Africa, ceded Surinam, and kept the New Netherlands. From the French England regained her West Indian possessions but lost Nova Scotia.

The disastrous end of the war had a dramatic effect on English politics, prompting Clarendon's dismissal, and a new period of bitter internal struggles in the government. Even greater, though, was its effect in continental Europe. Even before the war had ended, Louis XIV made a public announcement of his wife's claim to the Spanish Netherlands and sent his troops across the border. Methodically they set about reducing the fortresses in their path. The cool, calculated aggression of Louis XIV frightened all Europe. Louis' grandeur and ambition became the table-talk of England, as of all the continent: some wilder (and unofficial) French pronouncements saw him as the heir to the empire of Charlemagne – a claim to make the Hapsburgs furious, but also nervous; even in England the diarist and navy official, Samuel Pepys, speculated that if peace was restored between France and Spain, he 'will have nothing to do with his army unless he comes to us'.[20] The rearmament of the French navy from 1667 opened the worrying possibility that Louis aimed to challenge the English and Dutch naval duopoly, while the commercial offensive mounted by Colbert from 1667 was clearly directed at the exclusion of the Dutch and English from France's trade and encroachment on their own.[21] The French, Pepys thought, 'will undo us in a few years'.[22]

A small group of diplomats – the Dutchman Van Beuningen, the Austrian Lisola, the Englishman Sir William Temple, among others – urged a European alliance to curb his ambition. Lisola, whose pamphlet of July 1667, *Le Bouclier d'État*, accused Louis of aiming at a universal monarchy, continued tirelessly to try to create an anti-French coalition for the defence of the Spanish Netherlands. His master, the Emperor Leopold, however, gave up supporting his efforts in January 1668, and agreed to a treaty with France which effectively accepted Louis' claims in Flanders; the Dutch, despite their profound anxieties about French encroachment, even, at one point, suggested a partition of Flanders with France rather than risk war with Louis; and Charles II was in no financial position to join in the defence of Flanders, even if he had wished to do so: the war had left the government £2.5 million in debt and forced it into a programme of economy and reorganisation of its finances. Charles was suspicious, too, of any attempt by Louis and De Witt to partition Flanders.

All this makes it extraordinary that suddenly, in January 1668, he allowed himself to be persuaded into concluding a defensive treaty with the Dutch states-general, which included a commitment to force the combatants to accept peace on terms which Louis XIV had declared acceptable the previous September. A few days later Sweden joined the alliance as well, and eventually, though unwillingly, Louis agreed to the terms. At Aix-la-Chapelle in April the full treaty was finalised. For a few then, and rather more later, the Triple Alliance was a glorious instance of how protestant co-operation against the French menace could enforce a balance of power in Europe and bring Louis XIV to heel. Charles's sponsorship in February 1668 of peace between Spain and Portugal, and his appointment of Sir William Temple as ambassador to The Hague the same month seemed to suggest that the Treaty represented a permanent commitment to the anti-French coalition. In England however, the treaty failed at the time to receive the plaudits that the government expected: a lingering enmity to the Dutch, and the fact that the government refused to reveal its details dampened enthusiasm.[23]

The Triple Alliance and the Treaty of Aix-la-Chapelle were in any case far from perfect. It was probably not Sir William Temple's hope to arrest French expansionism, but the fear of a Franco-Dutch treaty and partition of Flanders which had persuaded Charles to agree to the treaty in the first place; moreover, it was clearly a very temporary arrangement, as the gains conceded to Louis in Western Flanders gave him ideal positions from which to mount a fresh attack, and the validity in principle of his wife's claim to the Spanish Netherlands had been recognised in the treaty. The impression of a firm alignment of England in an anti-French bloc was certainly false. When Louis, holding the Dutch responsible for the check to his conquests, turned away from the old Franco-Dutch alliance, Charles was delighted to resume the Anglo-French negotiations for a 'closer alliance', which had been going on since 1661. In 1669, the discussions assumed a new tone, after Charles sent, via his sister the Duchess of Orleans, his notorious undertaking to announce his conversion to catholicism. Nothing has caused so much of a problem in the interpretation of the reign as this undertaking. The most likely explanation still seems to be that the decision was connected in some way with the existing negotiations – as a way of securing the full attention and commitment of the French king, and distancing himself from the Dutch, it was unrivalled. But what precisely it was intended to achieve – whether he wished simply to further the 'closer alliance', to confirm Louis's abandonment of the Dutch, to obtain a more favourable attitude in other (especially commercial) negotiations, to wheedle a large subsidy out of France under false pretences, or to pave the way for a renewed war against the Netherlands – remains uncertain. Though the commercial negotiations ground to a halt over the next year, they did not create much of an impediment to the further development of the alliance; and it was the French who were more eager to put into effect the proposal mooted as long ago as 1667 of an attack on the Dutch – a proposal on which England stalled for a long time. Little can easily be concluded from the tortuous course of English diplomacy: the most sensible conclusion may be that it was pursuing many different objectives at the same time, and keeping open as many options as possible.[24] Over the year or more after Charles had declared his commitment to catholicism, the two countries conducted a complex and highly secret diplomacy which resulted in a private treaty signed in May 1670, committing England to join France in an attack on the Dutch; the French were to pay her subsidies of £225,000 each year during the war, which was to follow Charles's announcement of his conversion. Louis was to give Charles a further £150,000 in order to prepare for the domestic upheaval that was to be expected on the announcement. The beginning of preparations for war in June and July 1670 could scarcely be concealed, so a separate negotiation was begun, in which ministers not privy to the earlier discussions were involved. By December 1670 the 'Traité Simulé' was signed, containing the commitment to war against the Dutch and the French subsidies, but without the clauses concerning Charles's change of religion. The war, the parties agreed, should begin by May 1672.

There can be little doubt that, had the details of the secret treaty become public, they would have provoked an intense political crisis. The French alliance itself, when it became known, seems however to have caused little trouble in England. The Triple Alliance, however welcome to sophisticated pro-Dutch, protestant diplomats like Temple, had been treated with fairly general indifference: there is little evidence to show that the Dutch were yet generally seen again as protestant allies, rather than commercial enemies. Nevertheless, the government was cautious – and cynical – enough to seek money in late 1670 for preparations to support the Triple Alliance rather than for the new French alliance.

Over the following year or so, the Dutch tried to find out what was really going on in English foreign policy. While England stiffly resisted their attempts to strengthen the Triple Alliance, French diplomacy was active in Germany, suffocating with threats and gold any attempts to breathe life into a new anti-French coalition. The realisation in the Netherlands that the English and the French were planning a joint attack sent them deep into political crisis. England had her own, mainly financial, difficulties. In order to release sufficient money to pay for war preparations, the government was forced, on 1 January 1672, to declare the suspension of the repayment of all outstanding loans with the exception of those with specific statutory guarantees. The moratorium released funds of about £1.2 million – although it brought some of the London financial community close to ruin. In the run-up to the war, Charles II's undertaking to declare his catholicism was quietly dropped, although (partly, perhaps, with an eye to preventing Dutch attempts to play on English religious discontent) in March 1672 the government instead issued its new Declaration of Indulgence. Two days later, brushing aside the frantic efforts of Dutch diplomats to prevent it, Charles II declared war, citing Dutch resistance to English maritime sovereignty, obstruction to English fisheries on the East coast of England, disputes in the East Indies and Surinam, and abusive Dutch propaganda. Three weeks later Louis XIV followed suit.

Within a few weeks 120,000 French troops had marched through the Spanish Netherlands, up the Rhine and to the south-western borders of the Dutch federation, while his now ally, the Bishop of Münster, broke into the northern provinces – Groningen, Friesland and Overijssel. Within weeks, the Dutch were demoralised by the scale and speed of the assault, their country racked by dissension and factional hatred: in late August De Witt and his brother Cornelis, blamed for the success of the French, were seized by an orangist mob and murdered. Nevertheless, the French advance was halted, if only by flooding a line of defence which cut off the provinces of Holland and Zeeland from the invading army as well as from the other five provinces. The principal threat which England presented – of an attack from the sea – was more successfully prevented by the Dutch fleet, although it was helped by the lack of co-operation between the English naval commanders and their French allies. Above all, though, the Netherlands survived that season of terrible campaigning because on the removal from power of the De Witts, the Prince of Orange managed quickly, if tenuously, to assert his authority in what was left of the country. When the French offered terms, he rejected them.[25]

Once again, however, England was finding it acutely difficult to finance the war. Indeed, in the late summer and autumn of 1672 she tried to extract herself, hoping to gain an advantage from William's accession to power, and ever-suspicious that the French might make a separate treaty to England's disadvantage. There was not, though, much sign that William was willing to make peace on the sort of terms England would accept, and Charles had little choice but to continue fighting. To do so was growing equally difficult. The 1665–7 war had at least been undertaken with a large parliamentary grant; in 1672 there was nothing but the French subsidy, the ordinary revenue (with the temporary customs duties added in 1670) and the small subsidy granted in 1670. The government turned with some trepidation to parliament in the hope of setting the war on a firmer financial basis, its need more urgent because troops were being raised in England for a possible invasion of the Northern Netherlands. The session of parliament that opened in February 1673, though it objected to the new soldiers and the Declaration of Indulgence, showed little inclination to oppose the war itself. Although it was forced to abandon the Indulgence, the court won taxation worth £1.26 million to cover the following year's fighting. What was ominous for the government, however, was the level of public and parliamentary concern about the progress of catholicism at court: the rumours concerning the Duke of York and others which provoked the Test Act could have great repercussions on English foreign policy; for it was the suspected links between the French alliance and a catholic conspiracy – rather than the balance of power in Europe – that would make England turn decisively against the war, and against France.

The opportunity for a decisive victory was diminishing, in any case. In 1673, the allied fleet again failed to open the way for an invasion of the Netherlands by sea; the allies' suspicions of each other crippled their attempts to co-operate; and the Netherlands had begun to assemble a diplomatic defence. In October Spain declared war on France and England; by the end of the year the French had withdrawn from most of the Dutch republic; and at the same time, the Dutch mounted an extraordinarily successful propaganda campaign in England. In March 1673 (rather too late to influence parliament) Dutch agents had surreptitiously distributed large numbers of copies of a pamphlet entitled *England's appeal from the private cabal at Whitehall to the Great Council of the Nation, the Lords and Commons in Parliament assembled.* Picking up and amplifying French claims that the war was a war of religion, *England's Appeal* subtly insinuated that English ministers had corruptly and treasonably collaborated in Louis XIV's plans. It was of central importance in turning the English against the war; yet English opinion had already begun to connect the growth of popery in England with the assault on protestantism in the Netherlands. As evidence piled up, with the resignations following on the Test Act, of the conversion to Roman Catholicism of James and others in the government, the French alliance came to seem as if it had sapped English independence and undermined her religion. Radical criticism at the government's failure to take an independent 'English' line had existed for a long time. But the moderate language and strong message of *England's Appeal*, together with a huge print run, gave the argument the influence that it had never before had.[26]

It was not until parliament met again in October, however, that the war's opponents were able to exploit the growing protest against the alliance. As the new session approached, Dutch, Spanish and French agents furiously lobbied MPs. When parliament met its members were full of outraged nationalism and nervous protestantism. They bitterly attacked James's Modenese marriage, arranged with the help of France during the recess, and the war; they complained of French religious and commercial aggression; they pointed out how Spain's entry into the war would ruin the country's Mediterranean trade. They refused to grant more money until the expiry of the assessment given in the last session – which would not have been until August 1674. Neither a brief prorogation, while the king searched around for other solutions and unsuccessfully begged for French financial assistance, nor his promise in January 1674 to show parliament 'all' of his treaties with the French, succeeded in deflating the protest. Some now openly linked the French alliance with the

Stop of the Exchequer and the Declaration of Indulgence, 'which struck at all our laws, temporal and ecclesiastical, and all to countenance popery'.[27] Some MPs, coached by Dutch diplomacy, suspected the worst: Colonel Birch said, 'we have not had a smile since the French alliance began, and the second article of that alliance is to set up the Pope'.[28] When Charles received moderate peace proposals from the Dutch in the middle of January, he accepted the inevitable. In only four days, the Spanish ambassador in London mediated a treaty between the United Provinces and England. On 9 February the treaty was signed: almost the only concession England received from her two years' war and at the cost of a good deal of domestic discontent was an acknowledgement of the right of English naval vessels to receive the salute of Dutch ones.

England's foreign concerns were centred on Europe, yet they spread far beyond it. An increasing proportion of the government's time was spent in dealing with the affairs of its expanding territories and trade in other continents. By the 1660s nearly a quarter of England's imports came either from the Far East or the North American colonies; by the end of the century the proportion was to rise to one third (see table, p. 74). In the same period, the value of goods imported from the East Indies increased by 240 per cent. Between 1663 and 1681 annual imports of tobacco to London from America almost doubled: much of it was destined for re-export; imports of sugar, principally from Barbados and the other West Indian islands grew two-and-a-half times between the 1660s and the end of the century.[29] English traders were also slowly, but surely, establishing a trade in slaves in Western Africa. As Englishmen and women traded and established colonies across the world, successive governments were increasingly faced with the question of their responsibility for their protection, and of the relationship that should exist between such colonies and themselves.

England's trade may have been global, but the territories spawned by her émigrés were rather more concentrated. In the Far East, the Dutch prevented the English from establishing any permanent settlement or trading post; and in India, the East India Company had no ambition and insufficient power to carve out a territory for itself. In West Africa the Company of Royal Adventurers, then the Royal Africa Company, tried, but failed, to establish more than a foothold.[30] In the West Indies and in North America, however, Englishmen had secured a more enduring presence. English merchants had occupied a small collection of Caribbean islands in the 1620s and 1630s with little interference by the Spanish authorities: some, like Barbados, were uninhabited; others, such as Antigua, St Kitts, Nevis and Montserrat, were tiny. French and Dutch settlers had made similar settlements during the long wars of France and Spain. Although more and more sugar was grown on some of the islands, all lived to a greater or lesser extent parasitically on the Spanish colonies through smuggling and clandestine trade which sapped at the heart of Spain's colonial system; when Cromwell declared war on Spain the parasitism took the form of semi-official piracy. But the most populous and well-established settlements were in Northern America, on the Eastern Seaboard, from Virginia and Maryland in the South to New Hampshire in the North. In 1660, the English colonies had a population of perhaps 75,000. Their only close competitor was the small Dutch enclave of New Netherlands in their midst, centred on New Amsterdam, although in the North there were a few small French settlements established along the St Lawrence river.

The mother country's relationship with her far-away territories was a complicated and often awkward one. Distance, their conflicts of interest with the wider concerns of the English government, and the religious peculiarities of some of them made their relationship with the central government fraught with conflict and misunderstanding. Many of the colonies had been founded by corporations, such as the Virginia company; others had been established by individual grandees, equipped with royal grants of large tracts of territory (such as Lord Baltimore's colonisation of Maryland in the 1660s) or else simply by groups of men without particular royal sanction (like most of those in New England). A few, such as Jamaica, had been taken by conquest. All, however, had evolved similar governments, a tripartite division between governor (appointed normally by the Crown or proprietor, but sometimes elected), council and legislative assembly. Some acknowledged royal authority with various degrees of vagueness: a few virtually ignored the government in London.

In the 1650s the government had been most anxious to retain the English colonies within England's commercial ambit. The trend was maintained after the Restoration, in the Navigation Act of 1660, governing colonial trade, and in the several specialist councils for foreign plantations which were set up to handle colonial affairs. That which was established in 1670 was given powers 'to regulate the trade of our whole plantations, that they may be most serviceable one unto another, and as the whole unto these our kingdoms, so these our kingdoms unto them'.[31] In 1672 it was combined with the council for trade into a single body, under the presidency of the Earl of Shaftesbury; it was perhaps the high point of colonial policy, but even after Shaftesbury's dismissal in 1674 and the reversion of colonial affairs back into a committee of the privy council, the trend towards bringing the colonies into a more direct relationship with central government continued. The attempt to do so provoked numerous clashes with the colonial authorities, as did the government's efforts to regularise the defence of English North America by extracting taxes for the purpose from the colonists. Among the most obvious signs of independence, and of profound concern to a government worried by Dutch competition, was religious nonconformity. The colonies of New England were dominated by independents and presbyterians: Massachusetts, the strongest power among the confederation there, refused to acknowledge English sovereignty; the government was always nervous that it might lose its hold over the colony altogether. It was not, however, until 1677 that it despatched a commissioner to examine its government; and not until 1684 that it took action, removing the charter of the company that controlled the colony. Three years later a military governor was sent out by James II to take command of the whole of New England.

Further South, the Crown faced challenges to its control over the colonies when the corruption and incompetence of Sir William Berkeley, the governor of Virginia, provoked a rebellion which was only quelled by sending out a small military force in 1676. Elsewhere in the colonies, the government tried to prevent the growth of representative institutions. In 1682 it imposed on Jamaica a constitution like that of Ireland, in which the existing legislative assembly had no role in initiating legislation; a similar constitution was imposed on Virginia as well.[32]

The government began to look at England's colonies in more strategic terms. True, most of the English colonial system was upheld by private enterprise, and those most active in formulating the government's colonial policy were often those with considerable interests of their own in North America – men such as the Earl of Shaftesbury, Prince Rupert, the Earl of Sandwich and the Duke of Albemarle. But some of those responsible for the plantations saw the wider possibilities for English power in the West. In 1672, the council for foreign plantation's approval of attacks on Spanish, French and Dutch possessions was justified with the argument that 'they should ere long find it as great an affair of state to balance power in the West Indies, as it is now amongst princes in Christendom'.[33] In the 1660s, military men like the Duke of York and the Duke of Albemarle tacitly approved the unofficial war waged against Spain by the settlers of Jamaica. In the West Indies and North America they recognised the danger from France; the establishment of the Compagnie des Indes Occidentales in 1663 marked a new phase of French expansion in Canada and the beginnings of an attempt to create a system of intra-continental trade that threatened English power and commerce. The rising stakes in the international struggle for possessions and commerce across the globe had made the government concerned to protect and to profit from English private enterprise; the corollary was her heightened need to reinforce the authority of the Crown over its far-flung dependent – or almost independent – territories.

The one English colony in the Mediterranean – Tangier – had a more straightforward role, and a less complex, if no less eventful history. Given it as part of Queen Catherine's dowry in 1662, Englishmen saw Tangier as a fortress from which they might 'give the law to all the trade of the Mediterranean'.[34] With a powerful military base at the neck of the Mediterranean, England could cut the Dutch out of the area's commerce. It was far more easily boasted of than done. The harbour was never satisfactory, despite the time and money poured into improving it, and all the time it was threatened by the Moors. In 1680 the Moorish tribal leader, Abd Allah Gailan, mounted a massive attack on the town. English interests were better represented by the frequent presence of her navy in the Mediterranean: the importance of the Spanish trade and the Mediterranean carrying trade was recognised in the concentration there of naval power, designed to protect English vessels both from the privateering efforts of the European powers and also from the Turkish states of Algiers, Tripoli and Tunis, and the Kingdom of Fez, which preyed on Christian shipping. In 1671–2 an English fleet was sent against Algiers, in 1674–6 against Tripoli, in 1677–83 again against Algiers.[35]

By 1674, though, however essential these wars ultimately were for the confirmation of her naval power in the Mediterranean, England's political attention was fixed firmly on Northern Europe. The notion of a catholic, French and absolutist plot to deliver up England's independence, religion and liberties into the hands of Louis XIV had come, in a brief space of time, to the forefront of the political arena, and would dominate it for at least the next eight years. The events of 1672–4 had shown the volatility of public opinion and had demonstrated how effective foreign intervention in English politics could be. Foreign powers were not slow in recognising it, for even though England had pulled out of the war, the possibility remained that she might rejoin it. England's withdrawal had little effect on the course of the war on land. Having retreated from the United Provinces in 1673, the French made up for it by smashing into the Flemish lands of their new enemy, Spain, and by fomenting republican opposition to Prince William. The Dutch and Spanish appealed to the now virulently anti-French opinion in parliament in an attempt to coax England back into the war, on their side, as over the next two years the French advance steadily pressed forward into the Spanish Netherlands.

Those ministers most involved in the war had been dismissed, resigned or had lost their influence amid the protests and recriminations of 1673. The strongly anglican royalist ministers who replaced them mostly shared their countrymen's attitudes to France. Danby, the new lord treasurer, had views on foreign policy which were heavily influenced by those of the diplomat and opponent of French power, Sir William Temple, one of the architects of the Triple Alliance of 1668; in 1674 Danby sent him as ambassador to the United Provinces. Temple became closely identified with Danby's drive for a protestant alliance against France, which it was hoped would help to recreate the political unity and tranquillity of the nation, and by tapping nationalist and protestant sentiment, could restore England's power and reputation in the world. 'A king of England', Temple wrote to Ormonde in 1673,

> at the head of his parliament and people, and in their hearts and interests, can never fail of making what figure he pleases in the world, nor of being safe and easy at home; and may despise all the designs of factious men, who can only make themselves considered by seeming to be in the interest of the nation, when the court seems to be out of it.[36]

Charles, however, was not so sure. Increasingly concerned by domestic discontent, perhaps disturbed by the role of the Dutch in fomenting it, and certainly wary of again becoming embroiled in the European war, he clung to his friendship with Louis XIV. It took time, therefore, for any change in England's foreign policy to become evident, and even when it occurred, it was to represent a far from total commitment. The government instead relied in 1675 on its new religious policy to stem discontent when parliament met again; yet it found still much anxiety about a popish conspiracy and French alliance, bolstered by objections to the 4000 British troops which had been sent into French service at the peace, and joined now to economic attacks on France: in November 1674 English merchants protesting about the French government's restrictions on the cloth trade had drawn attention to England's unfavourable balance of trade with France.[37] Even when the government tried to signal its reversal of alliances in the autumn session of 1675 by requesting money to strengthen the English fleet against growing French naval power, parliament remained suspicious of a government whose conversion to the anti-French camp was so recent. The disappointing response confirmed Charles's preferences. In February 1676, despite Danby's obstruction, he concluded a formal but secret treaty with Louis XIV, in which he accepted French subsidies in return for delaying a further session of parliament. Parliament remained prorogued until February 1677, while the Dutch position deteriorated rapidly; in the campaign of early 1677 the French broke through William's defences and advanced deeper into Flanders.

Charles could scarcely resist for ever the pressure for a pro-Dutch foreign policy, particularly when it was joined – and to some extent encouraged – by his own ministers, and when Danby worked hard to reassure him that it was possible to keep parliament under control. When parliament met in February, the government accepted its demands for an English role in the protection of the Netherlands. But it refused to make any intervention before parliament had voted money for the purpose. It shortly became obvious that there was enough distrust of the government's intentions for the Commons to resist doing so until Danby gave clearer indications of progress in negotiations with the Dutch. The government was caught in a dilemma: it was reluctant to commit itself to any hostile action against France until it had made adequate military preparations; but without parliamentary supply, it could make none of the preparations which would persuade the Commons to open their purses. The Commons flew at the ministers for the delay. At the end of May they presented an address demanding, in the most direct terms, the completion of a Dutch alliance. By now, the government's patience – or at least the king's – was at an end. With the angry remark that 'you have intrenched upon so undoubted a right of the crown, that I am confident it will appear in no age (when the sword was not drawn) that the prerogative of making peace and war hath been so dangerously invaded', the king ordered the adjournment of parliament.[38]

The French, concerned that Charles had been wavering in his resistance to a French alliance, stepped in to suggest, via Ralph Montagu, the English ambassador in Paris, a new subsidy treaty. For once, the Dutch snatched a diplomatic coup from their hands, by reviving an earlier proposal, that Prince William should marry the eldest daughter of the Duke of York, Princess Mary. Why Charles, still in close touch with the French, should have agreed is uncertain, although he may have recognised an opportunity to capture power and influence in Europe by dictating a peace to the exhausted antagonists. It was a sudden and unexpected success for Danby and William, and as unexpected a shock for the French, when the prince arrived in London in October and the next month was married to his cousin. England agreed to press the French to accept the terms the Dutch offered, and when these, considerably more favourable to Spain and the Netherlands than the military situation warranted, were rejected in Paris, she immediately began preparations for war. Even this did not quite overcome parliamentary suspicions. When parliament met at the end of January 1678, the king's request for money for an army of between 30,000 and 40,000 to land in Flanders was still met with a series of frustrating difficulties: but in the end the government obtained a formal vote of £1 million, in February. Twenty regiments were raised and their embarkation for the continent began.

Charles's new alliance looked impressive, but it was soon undermined. France's sudden capture of Ghent in March, and of Ypres a few weeks later, produced almost irresistible pressure for peace in the Netherlands. Bypassing William and the English, Louis negotiated with the states-general; in May they accepted his terms. Pulling the rug from beneath Danby's feet, Louis began separate negotiations with Spain and with Prince William himself in June, leaving England trying to spring into a war which no longer existed. Charles himself accepted another secret treaty with Louis in May, promising once again a prorogation and the disbandment of his new troops in return for new subsidies. The English saw the whole fiasco as a conspiracy, planned by Danby, to create an army which could be used in England. Parliament demanded its immediate disbandment. Yet with many peace negotiations still unconcluded, the government was reluctant to lose its only diplomatic card. And the international situation had not lost its power to confuse English politics yet further: on the eve of signing peace with the Dutch, Louis demanded a delay until his ally Sweden could come to terms with her enemies. The move was widely interpreted as an attempt to complete some last minute military conquests. The Dutch, outraged, rediscovered the will to fight, and agreed with England on 16 July to continue the war if France failed to accept the peace terms already agreed. Twenty days after their deadline, Louis concluded peace, having failed to capture Mons. It was several days more before the guns fell silent, after William inflicted a parting defeat on the French; and it was months before the diplomats finally produced a general settlement, the Treaty of Nijmegen, in January 1679. Yet for the first time since 1672, Western Europe was now at peace.

The price of English involvement had been low in blood but high in money and in political capital. Although the Commons had voted £380,000 for disbanding the army, most of it had been used by keeping the 27,000 troops together during the crisis in July: with that money exhausted, and with the soldiers costing £158,000 a month, the government still needed more for their disbandment. Even after the sums given by parliament, the war had cost a further £1.38 million; the government's floating debt was now £2.4 million, and (not for the first time after an unsuccessful war) it faced bankruptcy. The mobilisation of 1678 may have prompted Louis to make peace, but in domestic politics it was an expensive failure. Rather than producing a wave of emotional protestant, patriotic sentiment, the intervention had resulted in confusion and in suspicion of England's diplomatic relationship with France, and of the militarism of her government.

By 1678 England's foreign relations were in chaos, and her politics at home in crisis. It was an ignominious end for Danby's hopes of a grand protestant, anti-French policy. England's ministers, claimed Andrew Marvell, corrupted by France, were conspiring to cut away England's liberties and her religion and to replace them with French slavery and catholicism: the final purpose of the whole project was to surrender England's independence to France. Marvell died in August 1678, too early to see the political crisis that followed the end of the European war, but there were others to echo his analysis. In verses on his death John Ayloffe, one of his political allies, wrote that England, from 'Europa's envy' had 'turn'd her scorn'.[39]

It was clear that Charles had become extraordinarily dependent on France, and was willing to ruin months of patient diplomacy with his instinctive preference for dealing with Louis XIV rather than the Dutch republic. Yet English policy had not always been so pacific, or so pro-French. In his earlier years Charles – and even more James – showed a genuine ambition to play a role in Europe, and a youthful belligerence. Both may have preferred alliance with the power and glory of the French monarchy, rather than with the bourgeois and pacific United Provinces, or indeed with the confused policy of a decrepit Spain. But neither was more devoted to the French alliance than it suited himself to be. Charles and James certainly failed to see, as diplomats such as Temple or Lisola saw, the need to maintain a balance of power in Europe and to curb French power. The complications of Dutch internal politics, however, made her a difficult partner; and throughout the period, ministers were always suspicious of Dutch republicanism and its role in arousing radical religious and political feeling in England. In any case, England was too suspicious of Dutch hankering after a French alliance to trust fully in them.

Despite his ambitions, Charles's search for power and influence in Europe had been a disaster. In the 1660s, it was defeated by a financial system which could not cope with a prolonged war; in the 1670s by a lack of political trust and goodwill. It had also held back England's recovery from civil war. The rapid expansion of trade whenever England was at peace – in the mid 1670s or the 1680s – showed the extent to which war retarded commercial growth. The strains which the wars imposed on government finances – even when adequate parliamentary funds were available – brought the government effectively to bankruptcy in 1667 and 1678, and forced it to cease the repayment of its borrowings in 1672. Financial problems left government at the mercy of parliament or in the pay of France; unsuccessful wars provoked recriminations and political crisis, and encouraged foreign powers to interfere in domestic politics, arousing unrest and stirring up factions. Charles's only achievement in almost twenty years of diplomacy was the impoverishment of his government and the suspicion of his subjects. By the late 1670s his foreign policy no longer had any other aim but to shore up his position within England itself. It had left the country and his power enfeebled as in 1678 it approached the greatest political storm since the Civil War.

5

FROM CONFLICT TO REVOLUTION: ENGLAND IN THE 1680s

By the end of 1678 the government's critics regarded the country as beset by powerful and unscrupulous enemies at home and abroad. Across the Channel sat Louis XIV, contemplating his next assault on European protestantism. In England they suspected misty conspiracies to sell the country's freedom to France and its religion to Rome. Corrupt ministers thumbed their noses at law and constitution, while toadying bishops abandoned the Church to its popish enemies. Most ominous of all, the large army raised early in the year still existed, the money voted for its disbandment spent on keeping it in being, ready to give the *coup de grâce* to England's liberties. Right at the centre of the corruption was Danby. It was not – yet – a general analysis, at least not all of it. Some of the former ministers (particularly Shaftesbury and Buckingham) who demanded Danby's head were too obviously self-interested; moderate anglicans might be alienated by the powerful whiff of anti-episcopalianism in the attacks; and however suspicious Englishmen were of catholic conversions, there was no clear evidence of the popish conspiracy that Marvell had written about. But over the six months that followed the end of the European war, all that changed: even moderate opinion came to accept the thesis that England's stability and independence were being undermined from within the government itself.

The presence of a large army in England during the summer and autumn of 1678 – some of it drawn from Ireland

– naturally gave rise to rumours and speculation. Few had any basis in fact, or were at all significant, but the evidence of a catholic plot that was brought by Israel Tonge and Titus Oates to the king and ministers about two months before parliament was due to meet again in October was more impressive. Their unusually detailed information had its confused origins in the foggy mind of Tonge, a former Oxford don and obsessive anti-papist, and the dubious imagination of Oates, a drifter, the son of an anabaptist, at one time an anglican clergyman and chaplain, and subsequently a catholic convert; but it had acquired a veneer of plausibility through Oates's eighteen months' acquaintance with Jesuit missionary circles on the continent, and a series of accidents which lent support to his accounts of a catholic conspiracy to assassinate the king and seize power. When he named Edward Coleman, a zealous catholic convert and secretary successively to the Duke of York and his wife, the privy council discovered that Coleman had been maintaining a treasonable correspondence with the French court concerning the promotion of catholicism and French interests in England; a few days before parliament was to meet, the magistrate before whom Oates had originally sworn the truth of his story, Sir Edmund Bury Godfrey, was found mysteriously murdered. Already public, Oates's revelations gained enormous credibility from Godfrey's death.

When parliament met, its members ignored the government's pleas for money for the disbandment of the army and demanded a proper investigation of the plot. London erupted with anti-catholic hysteria as Oates produced new information and new witnesses came forward to corroborate the story. The trial and execution of Coleman in November and December brought credence of the plot to a new height: Roger North wrote that

> the discovery of Coleman's papers made as much noise in and about London, and indeed all over the nation, as if the very cabinet of Hell had been laid open. . . . Peoples' passions would not let them attend to any reason or deliberation on the matter . . . so as one might have denied Christ with more content than the plot.[1]

In the first rush of panic, the government had difficulty in keeping control of parliament. Considering the government's response to the plot inadequate, the Commons assumed its investigation themselves. His enemies turned the anger directly at Danby: encouraged by France, the former English envoy in Paris, Ralph Montagu, showed the Commons evidence of Danby's participation (in fact unwilling) in the discussions earlier in the year over obtaining subsidies from Louis XIV in return for the prorogation of parliament. The House was outraged by this confirmation of Danby's long-suspected corruption: within two days, articles of impeachment for treason had been drawn up against him. A few days later the king, determined to avoid an embarrassing inquisition into the conduct of foreign policy over the past ten years, and finding its presumption less and less tolerable, prorogued parliament.

There was no alternative, though, to parliament as a source of money for the disbandment: the French had no wish to get Danby off the hook by providing more subsidies. The king instead resolved on a dissolution and a new parliament, offering the more moderate of the government's critics Danby's dismissal in return for his indemnity and a supply. The elections of February 1679, however, saw a powerful and spontaneous reaction against the court, and more seats contested than in any other election during the Restoration. When the new parliament met, it turned out to be even more determined than the old one to pursue both the plot and Danby: the moderates could not deliver what they had promised. When the king announced Danby's dismissal, but accompanied it with a full pardon, MPs were furious that those they held responsible for the plot could get off scot-free. Threatened with attainder, Danby surrendered himself, and was placed in the Tower of London. With Danby out of the way, the Commons became confident enough to vote £200,000 for the disbandment of the army: yet the leaders of the parliamentary protests made it clear that the corruption and conspiracy within the government did not begin or end with Danby; some claimed that they went right back to the

Restoration: 'when the king came home, his Ministers knew nothing of the laws of England, but foreign government'.[2] They turned to attack Danby's colleagues – above all, they attacked James, Duke of York.

James's conversion had formed the centre of anxiety about the country's protestant future at least since 1673. When Danby was the popular object of odium, in the later 1670s, interest in James dulled a little, but it was inevitable that a catholic plot, and the trial and execution of James's former secretary should turn attention back to the catholic heir to the throne, even if Oates and the others denied his personal involvement. It was not merely the prospect of James's succession that attracted hostility, although Charles's serious illness in August 1679 brought the possibility nearer. Ever since 1660 politicians had been wary of his military and authoritarian instincts. The Duke of York, Sir Thomas Player claimed, had 'concerned himself to model England according to his own turn. From whence came modelling the militia, the Justices of Peace, all the fortifications of England? Were they not of his modelling?'[3] As the popish hysteria inflated, Charles accepted the prudence of James's removal: the duke and duchess left for Brussels in early February. But the attack grew in their absence. 'I do believe', said Thomas Bennet, an associate of the Earl of Shaftesbury, 'that this plot had not been carried on without the Duke of York's approbation.'[4] In the ensuing debate there were suggestions of a regency should he succeed; even of his exclusion from the throne.

Charles tried to cool the political atmosphere by taking a number of the leaders of the opposition to James into the government. The Earl of Shaftesbury was made lord president of the council once more; moderate opponents such as the earls of Halifax and Essex in the House of Lords and lords Russell and Cavendish and Henry Powle in the Commons, as well as the deeply respected Sir William Temple, were brought into the privy council. It had little effect, however, either in building confidence in the government – because the king patently distrusted his new advisers and would not effectively co-operate with them – or in dividing its opponents.

On 11 May, after a report from its investigative secret committee on the extent of the Duke of York's involvement in the plot, the Commons voted to exclude him from the throne. Within a few days a bill to that effect had been read twice. Cutting short the bill and the prosecution of Danby, Charles prorogued parliament on 27 May.

The government was now under intense pressure. Despite the troops' successful disbandment, it remained in severe financial difficulties from which there was no prospect of relief (for Louis XIV seemed no longer to believe that he could derive any benefit by subsidising the English government) but by parliamentary grant. Charles needed parliament, but it was clear that parliament's demand for exclusion was implacable. Further complications were added when nonconformist resentment in Scotland bubbled over in May. The brutal murder of James Sharp, Archbishop of St Andrews, by conventiclers goaded to fury by the military suppression of nonconformity, provided the spark which encouraged nonconformists to armed resistance. Shortly after the murder, a group of conventiclers defeated government troops, and as large numbers came to join them, they marched on and occupied Glasgow. Once there, however, their unity and sense of purpose decayed, and a few weeks later the rebellion was decisively put down by troops commanded by the king's illegitimate son, the Duke of Monmouth, who followed military victory with an attempt to pacify the country using more liberal measures. The explosion of discontent into civil war had been averted – although for a moment the situation had threatened to resemble the Scottish war of 1639–40 which had provoked the English political crisis which followed it – but Charles was still left with the intractable problem of obtaining parliamentary supply without accepting exclusion: in the absence of any better proposal, he decided once more to dissolve the current parliament and try the government's fortunes again at a general election.

What was worse was that Monmouth's success in Scotland encouraged the revival of the old canard that Charles might be willing to substitute the popular and protestant Monmouth for the deeply unpopular James. When the king fell ill in August, some of his opponents feared that Monmouth planned to seize the throne on his death. James rushed back to London to secure his inheritance; his reunion with Charles confirmed the king's resolve to resist the calls for his exclusion. James was sent away again, but only to replace Monmouth in Scotland where he reversed his nephew's liberal policies and returned to repression, hunting down the radical remnants of the covenanting movement; Monmouth was despatched to the Netherlands, in disgrace.

The elections of August and September produced a parliament no less unruly than those in February. The king decided not to allow it to sit. He dismissed Shaftesbury and Monmouth from their offices; their supporters resigned from theirs and from the council. In December Charles announced that parliament would not meet at least until November the next year. The government issued a proclamation claiming that the plot had been fully investigated, and the conspirators dealt with. A crude attempt amateurishly engineered by a handful of catholics to discredit the exclusionists by inventing their participation in a supposed presbyterian and republican conspiracy to take over the government – the 'Meal-Tub' plot – was a messy failure, but at least showed the persistence of enthusiastic loyalism. A wave of publications sponsored by the Church and perhaps the government highlighted the implicitly revolutionary arguments of the exclusionists: they included a new *History of the Plot* by Roger L'Estrange, sniping by innuendo at the veracity of Oates's plot. Stimulated by such events and publications, some began to see the pursuit of the popish plot as dangerously destabilising, pushed on by those who were no friends to the monarchy.

Exclusionist arguments and exclusionist propaganda, however, far outweighed that put out on the other side. With the accidental lapse in 1679 of the Act which regulated the publishing trade, a torrent of pamphlets and books about the plot, dignified or scabrous, scholarly or scurrilous, poured from the presses. The stream of trials of catholics and catholic priests, many of whom were subsequently executed, was watched by a horrified but fascinated nation. Exclusionist politicians encouraged anti-popish demonstrations in London. In the absence of parliament they tried to stimulate other representative institutions to carry on the struggle against popery. In London, the struggles over the elections of sheriff, mayor and common council took on national political overtones. A group of peers, including Shaftesbury, opened a campaign of petitioning for the meeting of the new parliament. From December 1679 filled-in petition forms were being sent in from all over the country, and an enormous number of signatures were collected. The government remained adamant, however; it purged the commissions of the peace of many JPs who had supported exclusion or the petitioning movement; it canvassed for addresses of loyalty to counter the petitions; and it initiated a drastic programme of economy in its expenditure, under a new treasury commission headed by Lawrence Hyde. Even if it could not yet solve its financial problems, by the spring of 1680 the government was in a stronger position than at any time since 1678.

During the summer, however, anticipating a meeting of parliament in November, the exclusionists' leaders injected new excitement into the movement. Shaftesbury brought revelations of an Irish catholic conspiracy, hitting English anti-popery in its most sensitive place. When in May 1680 Charles again fell seriously ill, Monmouth's friends now claimed that he was in fact legitimate and the king's rightful heir, with or without exclusion. Most startling of all was Shaftesbury's extraordinarily cheeky attempt to have York indicted for catholic recusancy. The king was committed to holding a meeting of parliament in November; and parliamentary supply remained as necessary as ever, particularly when the government's finances were now rendered even more embarrassed because of the expected onslaught of the Moors against the Mediterranean outpost, Tangier. As the new session approached, the government began to disintegrate, as ministers tried to find ways of pacifying parliament and protecting themselves. Sunderland, the king's secretary of state, was negotiating with the exclusionists: even he now believed that Charles would have to accept James's exclusion from the succession.

When it met, on 21 October, parliament fell directly on the plot, listening avidly to new evidence from one of those concerned in the imposture of the Meal-Tub Plot who now found further invention the only means of self-preservation: Dangerfield said directly that James himself initiated an attempt on the king's life. An Exclusion Bill received three readings without even a vote. To the fury of the Commons, however, in the upper House, bishops, officers of state and dedicated loyalists combined to ensure its rejection by a majority of two to one. Despite the government's appeal to patriotic instincts, no money could be got for Tangier, or for anything else, without exclusion. In the second week of January 1681 the king prorogued parliament; a week later, he dissolved it, once again summoning a new one to meet at Oxford two months later.

By the end of the second Exclusion Parliament, the crisis was already more than two years old, and had shifted its attention firmly from Danby to James. Yet James was as much a symbol of the issues as the issue himself: the influence at court of popery, the government's alleged yearning for the freedom of absolutism, its enthusiasm for France, its favour for Irish catholics, its neglect of the old gentry of England. Popery lay at the heart of the plot. But although some of the brightest anglican and nonconformist minds were dedicated to attacking popery and rehearsing the arguments for protestantism, although popery was condemned as a barbaric religion whose practitioners 'eat their God', and 'make saints, then pray to them', the response to the crisis was not a particularly theological one.[5] The supposedly massive international effort of the Catholic Church, its vast reserves of cruelty and cynicism, were not seen as principally motivated by religious devotion. Controlled by the pope in Rome, the aim was temporal and avaricious: universal catholic domination. For Oates: 'Popery consists, in a word, in an Antichristian pretence of a Fifth Monarchical sovereignty over all the kings and princes of Christendom'.[6] The setting up of popery meant invasion: of property, by clerical avarice; of minds, by priestly tricks and fantasies; and of civil authority, by papal power.

The invasion was not merely metaphorical. The plot was believed to be constructed around an invasion and insurrection plotted by the pope. England would be attacked from Ireland and from France, for there was a close league between the papacy and France (it was claimed, in spite of the recent very public squabble of Louis XIV and Pope Innocent XI). England's new rulers would banish liberty and impose arbitrary government, for catholicism demanded obedience, crushing the individual conscience and independent thought, and the French monarchy ignored the laws and ruled by will alone. 'From popery comes the notion of a standing army and arbitrary power', claimed Sir Henry Capel.[7] And that claim brought attention back to the Duke of York: popish, absolutist and military. Many of the details of the Popish Plot seemed absurd: innocent, even naïve, elderly priests charged with conspiracy to murder the king, murder and treason; the contorted and confused stories of a succession of informers who ranged from the mad to the villainous; the extraordinary explanations concocted to account for Sir Edmund Bury Godfrey's death. But the anxiety – almost panic – over the Popish Plot reflects the profound nervousness pervading the country since the early 1670s over the survival of the English way of life. The plot drew together concerns which had worried Englishmen since the Restoration: the maintenance of the country's religion; her traditions of self-government; her integrity as a nation against foreign interference; the corruption of ministers; above all, the security of the law. The old system, constitution and hierarchy which conservatives – and the gentry in particular – had been trying to protect ever since the Civil War, seemed once more in imminent danger.

It was bad enough that some of the king's ministers already formed popery's fifth column within the government itself; worse still that the guardians of the protestant religion – the Church of England – seemed to exclusionists to be failing to do their job. Firstly, they obstructed Danby's prosecution in the House of Lords; then when James's exclusion was demanded, the Church, which had so resolutely defended monarchical legitimacy during the Civil War, could be true to its principles only by standing by James's right to the succession. Exclusionists bitterly censured 'a sort of clergy, ever since Archbishop Laud's time, too much addicted to popery', as Burnet wrote, 'a sort of men that for their own ends, and for every punctilio that they pretended to, would expose the nation and the protestant religion to ruin'.[8] In the Lords, the bishops blocked every attempt at exclusion. After the rejection of the Bill of November 1680, one balladeer complained

The grave House of Commons, by hook or by crook,
Resolv'd to root out both the Pope and the Duke;
But let 'em move, let 'em vote, let 'em pass what they will,
The bishops, the bishops will throw out the Bill.[9]

Partly in response, the pressure for exclusion took on a distinctly anti-episcopalian tone. Its opponents were christened 'tories', after the Irish catholic rebels of 1641. Nonconformists, and those who sympathised with them, had always been prominent in the attacks on Danby and James both inside and outside parliament: the parliaments of 1679 and 1680 had not reproduced the anglican royalist character of the Cavalier Parliament; many of the members of the Commons were concerned to bolster protestant unity in the face of the popish threat. Supporters of nonconformity introduced bills for the repeal of the Elizabethan Conventicle Act, for preventing penalties designed for catholics from being applied to protestant dissenters, and for the comprehension and toleration of nonconformists. The first passed both Houses, but the king prevented it being presented for his consent.

Charles's action was an indication of how suspicious the government had now become of protestant dissent. The parallels between the current situation and the protests of 1640 and 1641 were disturbing, and the government made sure, in publications that quickly increased in volume after 1680, that the public was aware of them too. The elegant but vicious polemic of L'Estrange was only the best of a growing number of satires and pamphlets which claimed that exclusion was but the dissenters' means to place themselves back in power. Exclusionists were caricatured as conventiclers, zealous troublemakers, presbyterians and sectaries: their enemies drew out to the full the hypocrisy they saw in their archetypes. They began to call them 'whigs', a term which indicated both their villainy and their roots in Scottish presbyterianism. What exclusionists wanted, they claimed, was nothing less than to dismiss the monarchy and revive the republic; their struggle had little to do with religious feeling, and everything to do with political radicalism and naked ambition. Underneath, they were no better than the papists.

The majority of 'whigs' could, and did, defend themselves by pointing out that they had no intention of diminishing royal power: if James was excluded, then his replacement would continue with such powers and prerogatives as Charles possessed. As they pointed out, the government's counter-proposal, to limit the catholic king's ability to make ecclesiastical, military and civil appointments, would have resulted in a far more considerable surrender of royal power. If such restrictions were to be imposed, Edward Vaughan argued, 'you take away all Royal Power, and make the Government a Commonwealth'.[10] There was nothing new, either, they argued, in changing the succession by act of parliament; it had been done in the reigns of Elizabeth and Henry VIII, among several others. To anglican royalists, their demand that parliament should alter the succession was outrageous. A monarchy whose sanctity had been considerably enhanced by the martyrdom of Charles I was not going to allow the divinity that hedged the king to be pulled down by act of parliament; in this refusal to secularise the institution of kingship anglican royalism made itself most powerfully felt. As Sir Leoline Jenkins, the secretary of state, argued in 1680: 'by the blessing of God, the king has not his Crown by designation; he is not an elective monarch'.[11] In Sir Robert Filmer's *Patriarcha* (a tract thirty years old, but now published for the first time), in Edward Bohun's *Defence of Filmer*,

William Sherlock's *The Case of Resistance*, in works by Nathaniel Johnston, George Hickes and many others, anglican royalists insisted that royal power and the right to it was derived from God, not from the community. As Filmer had notoriously argued, kings were metaphorically the fathers of their people, the successors of Adam, the progenitor of the human race, and the successors to the power that God had given him. To meddle with their right was a gross impiety. Some of them weighed in to revive the old constitutional debate as well. One of Filmer's other works, *The Freeholder's Grand Inquest*, first published in 1648, was also reprinted in the 1680s for its attack on the increasing claims of the Commons. Parliament and laws themselves owed their origin to royal concession, not to prescriptive right. What had been granted by the sovereign, such arguments signified, might also be taken away.[12]

Faced with these sort of responses, exclusionists were placed in an awkward position. Most of them sought only, in a moderate way, to prevent the appalling consequences they foresaw from the succession of a papist onto the throne of England. Few wished to face the theoretical implications of their action. Deeply attached to law and convention as the token of their security, they were reluctant to admit that the security they craved might only be found outside them. They may not have liked the high anglican royalist tone of the arguments of Filmer and his followers, yet within prevailing assumptions about government, it was difficult for any but the more radical to find ways of opposing their logic. Works like James Tyrrell's *Patriarcha non Monarcha*, Algernon Sidney's rambling *Discourses concerning Government* and John Locke's *Two Treatises of Government* did directly confront Filmer's central tenet, that the absolute right of kings was derived directly from God. Locke, Shaftesbury's aide and secretary, famously argue that political authority was a trust, given by a community to its rulers; should the trust be broken, authority would by right revert to the community. It was, in effect, a defence of rebellion against tyranny.

But neither Sidney's nor Locke's enormous, closely argued discourses were published in the early 1680s; had they been, many of the authors' fellow whigs would have been horrified by them: the majority of exclusionists saw their aim as preventing the violence and instability of popery, not as supporting the violence and instability of rebellion. Such a divergence, however, was virtually inevitable in a movement in which radicals and conservatives were combined, for the moment, in the pursuit of a single objective. For even at Westminster the exclusionists were never a 'party' in the modern sense, and exclusion was more of a sentiment than a movement. It had its leaders, of course, and the Earl of Shaftesbury was undoubtedly one of the most prominent and energetic of them, but he was only one (if the most inventive, admired and reviled) among several. Others, such as the Duke of Monmouth himself, the Earl of Essex, Ralph Montagu and Lord Holles co-operated with him, but only so far as suited their own aims. And the authority and standing of Shaftesbury, and his associate, Lord William Russell, in the House of Commons, was challenged and undermined by others, with different policies and priorities: men such as Silus Titus, Sir William Jones, Sir John Maynard and Sir Francis Winnington. Outside parliament, old republicans like Slingsby Bethel and Algernon Sidney were at least as influential as was Shaftesbury in arousing and manipulating popular feeling, and some more radical whigs were at least as eager to promote the wider attack on popery and arbitrary power and to insist on parliamentary and popular liberties as to focus more narrowly on exclusion.[13] Even exclusion itself, the apparently uncomplicated demand around which the whigs cohered, could divide them. For if James were excluded, who would replace him? Princess Mary, his eldest daughter, was heir presumptive to the throne, and her accession would bring to effective control of the government her husband and cousin, Prince William of Orange. But Charles's illegitimate son, the Duke of Monmouth, was a choice with far more popular appeal, represented in a torrent of pamphlets and newspapers as a protestant hero, whose bad relations with his uncle James made the nation's quarrel his own. For the moment, the question of which successor to choose was one which the more prominent of the whigs carefully avoided, but should exclusion succeed, it was one which might further smash the fragile unity of its protagonists.

Despite their disunity, the whigs came not only to dominate parliamentary business, but also highly effectively to extend the pressure on the king beyond Westminster, through the petitions of December 1679 to January 1680, and the two general elections of 1679 and the one in 1681, in which they succeeded in stimulating strong resistance all over the country to court candidates – even though in many places they failed to overcome the entrenched localism that had always influenced the outcome. The unusually democratic constitution of the City of London made it, too, a useful forum for whig protest. Its lord mayor, sheriffs, and the members of its legislative body, common council, were all chosen in regular elections, on a comparatively wide franchise. In 1679 and 1680 exclusionists stood for elections as sheriffs; in the latter year, both whig candidates were elected, and in 1680, too, the elections to common council showed the popularity in London of the whigs' cause.

For the government, London's whiggism was made worse by its lively radicalism. Some whig agitators, most notably Francis Jenks, demanded both an expansion of the popular element in the City's government and mandatory annual sessions of parliament.[14] London radicals provided much of the whigs' activist backbone. The twenty-nine radical or exclusionist clubs in London, some of them in existence as long ago as the mid-1670s, became the focus of their work. Some – the 'Green Ribbon' club in particular – seem to have had a major role in the production and distribution of exclusionist propaganda; others, such as the baptist Salutation Club, helped to inject venom and religious radicalism into the campaign.[15] London politicians had few of the qualms of country men about exploiting popular discontent. They directed their propaganda to the widest possible audience, helping to organise the massive demonstrations on important anniversaries in the protestant calendar when effigies of the pope were paraded through the streets and then burnt. The vast crowds which attended such events – 200,000 people were said to have witnessed the procession in 1679 – though largely good-humoured, recalled the rioting of 1641 and carried the implicit threat of uncontrollable violence. The government was worried, but nervously moderate country whigs may not have been happy either.

Popular political sentiment was far from entirely exclusionist – there is plenty of evidence of popular hostility towards the whigs, and of considerable sentimental monarchism – yet the government and tory propaganda firmly and successfully associated whiggism with populism.[16] Tory satirists savaged popular ambitions and pretensions to politics: 'Each cobbler's [a] statesman grown, and the bold Rabble/Convert each Alehouse Board to Council-Table'; exclusionists wished to 'teach the Nobles how to bow/And Keep their Gentry down/. . . The name of Lord shall be abhorr'd/For evr'y man's a Brother'.[17] The populist, metropolitan part of the whig movement may have been particularly effective in maintaining the excitement and momentum of exclusion when in the absence of parliament it might have decayed; yet its methods risked alienating the more moderate exclusionists on whom whigs had to rely for their real political influence. The divergent tendencies within whiggism might ultimately pull it apart; in the next two or three years, the king, his ministers and propagandists, worked hard to provoke them to do so.

They were helped by a gradual improvement in the government's financial position. In early 1681 the government was still in very dire financial straits: yet with an English victory in Tangier at the end of October and a peace treaty with the Moors, and with severe cuts in government expenditure, some of the financial pressure had been taken off the government. To add to this, France began to reconsider her refusal of aid to Charles II. Louis XIV's interventions in English politics had always been designed to secure his freedom of movement on the continent, and more specifically, in recent years, to try to prevent Prince William of Orange from forming an alliance which might threaten his ambitions in Flanders and Germany. To that end, from 1678 his ambassador in London had been active in distributing to the court's opponents money and cynicism about the government's intentions in preparing for war with France, while Louis withheld money from Charles, and subsidised Danby's enemies, in order to secure the lord treasurer's downfall. The growth in the stridency of whig demands, however, may have given him cause to reconsider, but more to the point were the signs that Charles II was trying to revive the card of a protestant foreign policy in order to overcome his domestic crisis. He knew that Lord Sunderland, the secretary of state, was discussing with foreign diplomats the means of resisting French incursions in Germany; that in the summer of 1680 England concluded a treaty with Spain; and that one of Charles's increasingly influential advisers, the Earl of Halifax, although no exclusionist, was known to be deeply in the Prince's interest. Louis XIV was finally induced to offer a resumption of his subsidies to Charles II. In March 1681 a new agreement was signed by which he would send Charles £115,000 a year for three years, plus £40,000 immediately, on his abandonment of the Spanish treaty. The sum was small, but the agreement coincided with the expiry of a ban on trade with France, imposed in 1678. Almost immediately, English trade in Europe flourished, bringing with it an enormous expansion of the customs revenue, by almost £140,000 a year. Aware of the passing of the worst of its financial problems, the government could more confidently face a new meeting of parliament.

The elections of early 1681 had produced a parliament little different from those which preceded it: there could be little doubt that it would once again demand the Duke of York's exclusion. The king, however, signalled his determination to resist it, even if, as the government seemed to expect, it might provoke disorder, even rebellion. He dismissed the councillors who had shown support for exclusion – including the Earl of Sunderland – and replaced them with firmly reliable anglican royalists. The parliament was convened not to London, where the possibility of a riot was a very real one, but to Oxford; the permanent military presence in London was strengthened and almost 700 soldiers were sent to Oxford. The whole country's attention was concentrated on the meeting; the exclusionists stimulated a fresh round of addresses from their constituencies to whig MPs, requesting not only exclusion, but in some cases annual parliaments. And they found a new informer, Edmund Fitzharris, to testify, entirely falsely, about York's attempts to assassinate the king.

The third Exclusion Parliament lasted almost exactly a week. When it met, it quickly revived the exclusion bill; Charles, almost as quickly, dissolved it. A week after its dismissal, Charles issued a declaration explaining his actions, appealing to royalist, conservative and anglican opinion: 'who cannot but remember', it asked, 'that Religion, Liberty and Property were all lost and gone, when the monarchy was shaken off, and could never be reviv'd till that was restored'.[18] Ordered by the archbishops to be read in all parish churches, the declaration was an effective response to the widely disseminated whig literature: whig responses bitterly attacked it and the legality of the dissolution. The government followed it up by stimulating addresses from the country thanking the king for his declaration. It struck, too, at the whig propaganda machine: in April the whig printer Francis Smith was arrested; several other printers were later indicted. The king seemed determined to assert his authority.

The whigs responded by turning to the City. They succeeded, by a small majority, in obtaining the vote of common council to request the king to call a new parliament, and in the shrieval elections in June the court's candidates were soundly beaten. The victory was crucial in the next moves in the government's attempt to regain political control, for the sheriffs were responsible for nominating grand juries in London; if the government made any attempt to put whigs on trial, whiggish grand juries could form a considerable obstacle. Two minor figures in the whig propaganda machine, Stephen College and John Rouse, had already been arrested at the end of July. College was charged with plotting rebellion after the Oxford dissolution: when a whig grand jury in London refused to commit him for trial, the government transferred his case to

Oxford, where he was safely tried and hanged. Shaftesbury had already been arrested: but the evidence against him was so poor that there seemed little point in removing the case to Oxford, so that when on 24 November a whig grand jury found Shaftesbury innocent of plotting rebellion and the deposition of the king as he was charged, the government could blame them, not its case, for the defeat. Shaftesbury was released a few days later, as London crowds celebrated the outcome with bonfires and demonstrations.

The government's campaign against the whigs continued nevertheless. Propagandist attacks on Shaftesbury were stepped up: Dryden's *The Medal* alleged that Shaftesbury had preached to the crowd '. . . that Power is lent,/ But not conveyed to Kingly government', and maintained that '. . . the multitude can never err'.[19] The government initiated a general persecution against the nonconformists, and began proceedings to recall the City's charter, which might enable it to impose new rulers on London. It was to be a long process, but in the meantime it tried other ways of capturing control of the City. It revived an ancient claim that the lord mayor should nominate one of the two sheriffs, and caused popular uproar when in the two subsequent elections, the incumbent sheriff declared the tory candidates elected. At the election of the lord mayor in October 1682, the government also ensured the success of its choice. By the end of the year it was in effective control of the executive of the City and – ominously for the remaining whigs – of the London grand juries.

The danger for whigs – and the imminence of their final defeat – was clear. The day after the new sheriffs were sworn in, Shaftesbury went into hiding: at the end of November, already ill, he left for the Netherlands. Two months later he was dead. That the whigs had by then been effectively pushed out of the mainstream of politics was suggested by the fact that even before his departure, they had been toying with plans for a rebellion. Monmouth's tour of the north-west of England in September 1682 had already shown the desire of some of them to demonstrate their enormous appeal among the common people – for Monmouth's huge personal popularity was made evident in the enthusiasm of his reception. The government had been alarmed enough to place Monmouth (briefly) under arrest, but as it later discovered, Monmouth's semi-royal progress was innocent in comparison with what others may have been contemplating. The evidence is difficult to interpret, but in 1683 the government believed that it had found strong, if confusing, evidence that Shaftesbury, Monmouth, Russell, Essex and Lord Grey, together with the Scottish Earl of Argyll, had been in late 1682 discussing simultaneous risings in London, the country and in Scotland. London radicals were heavily involved. There may also have been a separate, extremists' plan for the assassination of Charles and James. It seems certain that there had been more than vague talking among the principals, and after Shaftesbury's death more conspirators were drawn in, including perhaps Algernon Sidney and the MP John Hampden. By June 1683 the government possessed firm information about the so-called 'Rye House Plot' to assassinate the king and duke. At the end of that month, it arrested many of the whig leaders – Russell, Sidney, Essex, Hampden, and Howard of Escrick. Others, including Monmouth himself, went into hiding. Essex was found dead in the Tower, presumably a suicide, though the whigs claimed it was murder. Howard of Escrick turned king's evidence, and provided some of the information needed to convict Russell of treason. But the vagueness of the conspiracy made it difficult to secure further convictions. It was not until the discovery of Sidney's manuscript *Discourses concerning Government* with its defence of resistance against the monarch and of tyrannicide, that the government could put together a charge of treason against him. He was executed in December. Against Hampden, however, the government could bring no capital charges.

The evidence that there had been a fully-fledged plot for a rebellion may not have been very good, but the proof that the whigs had at least contemplated moving from political action to actual violence was precisely what the government needed to poison the remaining support for their cause. Even former exclusionists like Lionel Ducket, an MP for Calne in

Wiltshire, now condemned the old whig leadership: 'it is plainly evident that too many of them had at that time designs in hand more wicked, than their malice could invent to accuse the papists of'.[20] The government took full opportunity of popular, and especially gentry, disillusion with whiggism. It now brushed aside the City's attempts to defend its constitution, revoking and eventually remodelling its charter, diminishing its right to elect its own officers. Action against other boroughs followed. A few had already received new charters with similar changes; now many more writs of *quo warranto* were issued. Within a year twenty-four corporations had new charters. In the five months after that thirty-two were remodelled. Often the changes were small in scale, simply the insertion of clauses which allowed the Crown to veto new members of the corporations, but in effect they allowed the Crown rather greater influence over these alternative centres of political life.[21] The discovery of the plot also delivered an enormous stimulus to the persecution of dissent on which the government had embarked in 1681. Where in Hampshire in 1682 convictions of protestant dissenters had been principally of quakers, in 1683, they included all types of dissenter.[22] The more determined tories broke up dissenters' meetings all over the country, smashing up their meeting houses and arresting the offenders. Purges of whigs from local offices had begun as long ago as early 1680; there were more comprehensive purges in the spring and summer of 1681, when a council committee was established to review all the commissions of the peace and lieutenancy. Further changes to the commissions of the peace followed in 1682 and 1683.[23]

This collection of moves against dissent and whiggism is usually referred to as the 'Tory Reaction'. It is difficult to judge, however, how far they resulted from the pressure of local tories, and how far they were planned and initiated by the government. Undoubtedly old anglican royalists, whose hand the government had stayed so often in the past, relished the prospect of firm action against the old parliamentarians and dissenters who (many of them felt) were pushing them from local prominence. Many of the *quo warranto* writs against borough charters were issued in response to the requests of local tories struggling against a whig (and often dissenting) town corporation which they could do little on their own to remove. In some cases, local tories had to apply a good deal of pressure before the government accepted the need for a new charter.[24] When they came, the purges tended to be fairly moderate: no more men were removed than was sufficient to give the tories the balance of power, and the government was reluctant to remove whigs who were powerful and respected figures in their communities.[25] It was constitutionalist, legalist government tories, such as Lord Guildford, the lord keeper, and Secretary Jenkins, who guided the process: none of them, at least until 1685, seems to have regarded the corporation purges primarily as a means of ensuring a quiescent parliament; neither did they – until late 1684 – themselves initiate the proceedings against most of the corporations. Yet the government was not merely the passive agent of a gentry reaction. It was the government that had deliberately stimulated gentry fears of political violence and social subversion. Neither was it simply a 'tory' reaction. The failures of persecuting anglicanism before the 1680s were largely due to the inactivity, or obstruction, of justices and other law officers who were largely indifferent to the progress of nonconformity: if persecution was now more successful, it was at least in part due to those moderates who, frightened by the whigs, no longer stood in its way.

Toryism, in any case, was no more of a unified movement than whiggism had been. The reaction against whiggism was provoked by a horror of violent political change: it did not simply show that the nation thoroughly approved of the Duke of York's politics or his religion. Even within the tory-dominated government, there were deep divisions that dated back to the beginnings of the exclusion issue. Halifax, one of Charles's closest advisers, was reputed a moderate – more determined tories disgustedly condemned him for 'trimming': he had been one of the authors of the proposal to place limitations on James's power as an alternative to exclusion, and his friendship with William of Orange – who had often been mentioned as replacing James in the succession should an exclusion bill pass – made him deeply suspected by the Duke of York. There were the old anglican royalists, bred in the Civil War: the now very old Duke of Ormonde, Guildford and Jenkins. And there were those with whom James himself was closely associated: his brother-in-law, Lawrence Hyde, now Earl of Rochester, or the Earl of Sunderland (despite his one vote for exclusion, and despite his enmity with Rochester). When in May 1684 the Duke of York was restored to the privy council some of the divisions emerged. There were disagreements over Europe: Halifax tried unsuccessfully to encourage the government to give closer support to William of Orange in his efforts to resist Louis XIV. He also aroused York's fury when he attempted to effect a reconciliation between the king and Monmouth. York himself disturbed the older royalists with the ways in which he and his allies, Sunderland and Lord Chief Justice Jeffreys, pressed for the lifting of the recusancy laws from catholics. Older tories – particularly Guildford – were equally doubtful about the way in which at the end of 1684 Jeffreys put new vigour into the issue of *quo warrantos* and the surrender of corporation charters. Halifax bitterly opposed the decision not to hold a meeting of parliament in 1684 when, according to the 1664 Act repealing the Triennial Act, one ought to have been held. York's associates strengthened their hold on government: Sunderland replaced Lord Conway as secretary of state, and the Duke of Ormonde was removed from the lord lieutenancy of Ireland. A catholic, Richard Talbot, later Earl Tyrconnell, came to possess the most influence in the government of Ireland.[26]

In any case, James was soon to get control of the entire government. On 2 February 1685 the king suddenly fell ill. A few days later he died, leaving the nation in the hands of the popish successor whom it had dreaded for so long. Yet what ought to have been a crisis seemed a curious anti-climax. James took pains to emphasise the continuity of his rule with that of his brother: his council included much the same people as Charles II's; even Halifax was retained as its lord president. The new king gave guarantees before the council, which were subsequently published, 'to defend and support' the Church, never to 'invade any man's property', and to 'go as far as any man in preserving' the nation 'in all its just rights and liberties'.[27] With the announcement of a new parliament, the declaration gave a considerable degree of assurance; but the orders to the Archbishop of Canterbury, William Sancroft, to prevent any preaching against the Roman Catholic Church, and the king's hint that his continued support for the Church of England could be conditional on its compliance were less encouraging. The king's sponsorship of catholic literature – and above all the publication of a pamphlet, purporting to be written by Charles II, approving Roman Catholicism – came as a shock, and began to give some indication of the strength of James's commitment to his self-imposed task of re-establishing catholicism in England.

James's determination to achieve this had been formed a long time ago. His conversion, around 1668, had been courageous, even quixotic – an indication of the man's almost heroic firmity of purpose. But how honest, how simply religious, was it? Whigs tended to see James's Roman Catholicism as of a piece with his natural authoritarianism; and indeed James, like Charles, undoubtedly believed that the Roman Church's principles of religious authority presented a far better foundation for monarchical power than the more complex notions of religious authority held by the Church of England. And James's distaste for religious coercion, his willingness (later on in his reign) to grant freedom of worship to nonconformists of all kinds, hinted that he had reached the same conclusion as (apparently) had his brother: that religious pluralism permitted the monarchy to retain far more power than did a monopolistic national church – however much that Church theoretically acknowledged the Crown as its supreme head – although he remained deeply suspicious of what he regarded as the dangerously anti-monarchical principles of some nonconformists, particularly presbyterians. But James's obvious piety and his profound sense of God's guidance suggest far more than a political dedication to his Church: there can be no doubt not only that he was sincere in his object of reviving the Roman Catholic Church in England, but also that he saw it as the principal task of his reign.

The king recognised that the permanent re-establishment of catholicism in England would require enormous reserves of patience in both time and temper. He recognised, too, that it would be impractical as well as contrary to his revulsion for the forcing of conscience to attempt to reconvert England by force. Unfortunately, James was blessed with little patience, and the catholics who surrounded him and pressed him on with boundless enthusiasm – his devout wife, Mary of Modena, and his enthusiastic jesuit confessor, Edward Petre, among others – had even less. James's determination to restore catholicism to England took up most of his energies, and there is no evidence (as whigs claimed there was) that he also cherished an overarching ambition to crush English liberties. Yet his autocratic instincts had been reinforced by the experience of the exclusion crisis, and there can be little doubt that if James meant to do anything, he meant to ensure that his authority was properly felt within the country. His contempt for and dislike of parliament was clear: both the king and his ministers discussed with the French ambassador means to enable the king to rule without recourse to it.[28] Right at the beginning of the reign, his decision to order the continuation of the customs and excise revenue before the normal parliamentary sanction was received seemed to be an indication of a willingness to ignore constitutional convention in a search for independence. The unusually strenuous efforts of the government to secure the return of satisfactory members showed that James's ministers would be more active even than Danby in intervening in parliamentary business.[29]

Little could be expected of James in handling foreign affairs. However patriotically belligerent he had been in the past, foreign involvements were now a distraction from his domestic objectives. His attitudes were as ambivalent as his brother's had been. Louis XIV was careful to establish good relations with James, reviving payments that were still owed under the

1681 subsidy agreement with Charles, and James was naturally inclined to friendship with a king whose Roman Catholic
zeal was scarcely paralleled. Yet he also felt a family loyalty to
William of Orange, his son-in-law. It was difficult to balance
the two at a time when Louis was doing his best to undermine
William's authority in the Netherlands, and cut off the
revenue he derived from his small principality of Orange, in
Southern France. In August 1685, James renewed the 1678
alliance with the Netherlands, and soon Louis and his
diplomats were beginning to revise their views of the
significance of James's accession. James was never, though,
really confident of William as an ally: the prince's contacts
with the whigs worried him, and he largely kept out of
William's dispute with France. There were more important
things to do at home.

James could take both encouragement and warning for the
success of his project from the result of the elections of March
1685. It was principally a genuine revulsion against whiggism
that produced a deeply tory parliament. Only about fifty-
seven men who had been identified with the whigs were
elected. Yet some of the success had to be attributed to
Sunderland's energetic electioneering and Jeffrey's efforts at
remodelling borough charters, which may have been responsible for the unusual youth and inexperience of many of the
new parliament's members.[30] Many old tories were dissatisfied.
John Evelyn complained of the election of 'very mean and
slight persons (some of them gentlemen's servants, clerks, and
persons neither of reputation nor interest)', and when parliament sat, old MPs such as Sir Edward Seymour and Sir John
Lowther protested against the government's interference.[31]
Nevertheless, the parliament, fortified with James's assurances
of the position of Church and law, seemed eager fully to
cooperate with the king. James was given the same permanent
revenues which Charles had enjoyed, and the Commons voted
additional customs duties for eight years in order to pay off
the debt inherited from Charles II. On other matters,
however, the Commons were less amenable. A vote by the
committee of religion to request the king to put into force the

laws against all dissenters, including catholics, was distinctly unwelcome, and the king succeeded in getting the whole House to reject it; but it did reveal a galling, stubborn opposition to his hopes.

Such thoughts were set aside, however, in a wave of tory unity when news reached London of the landing of the Duke of Monmouth at Lyme Regis in Dorset, and his gathering together of an army to oppose the king. Monmouth's rebellion had its origins in the conspiracies surrounding the Rye House Plot: many of those who had fled to the Netherlands at the time of its discovery had continued in exile to plan a revolt. Even so, they were poorly prepared for one. The Scots had been much more active: by the time of Charles's death the Earl of Argyll's plans for a landing and rising in Scotland were already quite far advanced. Not until March did Monmouth finally agree to join in the enterprise, and from April both Scots and English rebels were meeting regularly, buying arms and preparing ships, and trying to secure promises of help from England, while evading, with the collaboration of the Dutch local authorities, the efforts of the English government to obstruct them. On 2 May Argyll sailed – a month later Monmouth followed, landing on 11 June. By that time Argyll's ramshackle rebellion had already been defeated, and he captured. Monmouth's luck and management were better. As he marched North, aiming for Bristol, he caught the imagination of the youth of Somerset and Dorset. He collected an army of perhaps 3000–4000 men: despite its inexperience, indiscipline and the inadequacy of its armament, it captured Taunton with scarcely any resistance from the local militia. In London, parliament rushed through an Act of Attainder outlawing Monmouth and voted an extra £400,000 worth of customs duties to defray the cost of defeating him. The government, at first taken aback by the rebellion's success, in a few weeks doubled the size of the army, and a large body of regular troops was sent down to Somerset. Even this narrowly escaped a spectacular defeat: on the night of 5/6 July Monmouth nearly succeeded in pulling off a surprise attack. But the attack went wrong, the surprise was lost, and in the ensuing fight before dawn 1300 or so of the rebels were massacred. The massacre continued for several months: another 1300 were captured and tried, and many of them were executed. Many more were transported and sold as labourers in the plantations. Monmouth himself was captured and executed, nine days after the battle of Sedgemoor.

The support that Monmouth's rebellion received testified to the depth and bitterness of the fear of popery among common people. It did not testify to support for dissent: there were some dissenters in the rebel army, but not a disproportionate number. More prominent dissenters – even quakers – studiously avoided involvement. [32] But tories had contracted a deep enough prejudice against dissent to hold them largely responsible. James himself, and others, labelled Monmouth a 'downright enthusiast', and saw his rebellion as inspired by nonconformists. In the second half of 1685 there was a fresh wave of persecution of dissent. For the tory gentry, it had been an instructive reminder of the bloody instincts of nonconformity, but it had been particularly alarming to see how nearly the rebellion had succeeded. John Evelyn wrote that 'such an inundation of fanatics and men of impious principles must needs have caused universal disorder, cruelty, injustice, rapine, sacrilege, and confusion, an unavoidable Civil War, and misery without end'. [33]

For the king, the rebellion had demonstrated both the strengths and the weaknesses of his position. His most obvious weakness was the military one. The failure of the militia in the rebellion convinced him of the necessity of increasing his regular forces: the troops raised to defeat Monmouth were retained on the permanent establishment and further recruitment added more. By the end of the year James possessed an army of about 20,000 men. Parliament, when it resumed after its summer recess, could hardly be expected to welcome the new troops, let alone the catholic officers or the infringement of the Act. James's request for a further grant to pay his new forces met immediate opposition. Older tories, such as Sir Thomas Clarges, Sir William Twisden, Sir Edmund Jennings or (in the Lords) Halifax, Devonshire and Bishop Compton, objected vigorously to the breach of the Test Act – 'a breach of our liberties' according to Clarges, and the first step in the creation of a popish standing army. 'Supporting an army is maintaining so many idle persons to lord it over the rest of the subjects. . . . And for officers to be employed not taking the Tests, it is dispensing with all the laws at once.'[34] Even so, the Commons approved an extra £700,000 for the government's needs (although it was £500,000 less than it had asked for); but with it, they voted an address pointing out the illegality of the employment of catholic officers. Only by repealing the Test Act could it be legally justified. James was incensed at the address: abandoning the money, within two days he had prorogued parliament. A day later, as if in an act of defiance, he dispensed with the provisions of the Test Act for sixty-eight catholic officers.

As the Commons had implied, the legality of such dispensation was disputable. James felt there was a good enough case for it to attempt its vindication in the courts. A test case was arranged, in which a catholic officer, Sir Edward Hales, defended himself against an action based on the Test Act, pleading the king's dispensation. The most recent judgement on the royal power to dispense with statute, of 1674, had seen as acceptable a royal dispensation which did not damage the interests of any particular individual. Yet this judgement still left a considerable degree of room for argument, and to obtain a suitable verdict in the Hales case James had to remove two judges in February and a further four in April. Thus purged, out of the twelve judges who heard Hales's case on appeal in June, only one refused to accept the government's argument: the dispensing power had been vindicated.

It was a pyrrhic victory: James's enthusiasm for the army had already made him seem to be behaving arrogantly towards parliament; now the law, too, had been made to serve his purposes; within a little time even the sanctity of private property would appear to be subordinated to his wider aims. The difficulties of accommodating an army so rapidly expanded forced its commanders into billeting their troops illegally on private citizens. More sinister than such casual infringements of private rights were the occasions when troops were deliberately quartered as a punitive or cautionary measure. In early 1686 troops were billeted in dissenters' meeting houses in the City of London; even in the 1685 elections the threat of quartering had been used to help persuade recalcitrant voters. The great summer exercises which James held for a large part of his army generally at Hounslow Heath in Middlesex displayed the military power of the Jacobean state to those who doubted the king's capacity, or will, to enforce his authority.

The defeat of the rebellion had anyway convinced James of his one, overriding strength – the approval of God – and had confirmed his determination to press ahead with his plans; with God's approbation, he was invulnerable to his enemies. Moderates were removed from his counsels: Halifax for his defence of the Test Act; Bishop Compton of London for his opposition to the granting of army commissions to catholics. In January 1687 the king finally dismissed his brothers-in-law, Rochester and Clarendon, despite their desperate attempts to retain their posts. In their place, James brought men with a greater commitment to his plans for the re-establishment of catholicism. The catholics Arundel, Bellasis, Powys and Dover came into the privy council; Lord Tyrconnell finally became lord deputy of Ireland, Arundel became lord privy seal; Sunderland took Halifax's position as lord president besides retaining the secretaryship; Jeffreys, protestant but pliant, was advanced to the post of lord chancellor on the death of Lord Keeper Guildford.

The catholicising of the English government was a frightening step, particularly when compared with events in France. In 1679, Louis had stepped up his campaign against the protestants, until in October 1685 he revoked the Edict of Nantes, the law which had guaranteed the rights of Huguenots. Half a million of them fled, many of them to Britain, shocking their co-religionists with stories of French catholic oppression and cruelty. James suppressed the details in newspapers and pamphlets, and tried to stem the tide of anti-catholic comment that followed. In early 1686 he issued a directive against seditious and controversial preaching; when he ordered the suspension of one London clergyman who was deemed to have contravened the guidelines, Bishop Compton refused to put it into effect. In response, James created a commission for ecclesiastical causes, which (to James's opponents) appeared similar to an institution used by Archbishop Laud in the 1630s and abolished by parliament in 1641. The commission suspended both the clergyman and Compton himself in what was seen as an extension of royal authority over the Church with unpleasant implications. At the same time the government planned to bring catholics into local and national offices. In October 1686 it established a committee to oversee the inclusion of catholics and other amenable men into the commissions of the peace. In January fresh commissions were issued including nearly 500 new JPs: 64 per cent of them were catholics. Almost 250 old JPs were left out, many of them of high social status. The new JPs were dispensed from the requirement of swearing the Oaths of Allegiance and Supremacy. Old tories such as Evelyn condemned the new appointments as being drawn from 'the meanest of the people'.[35] Ireland provided a breathtaking illustration of how far the infiltration of catholics could be taken. With the arrival of Tyrconnell in Dublin as lord deputy, the campaign to bring a catholic character to government institutions was accelerated. By the autumn of 1687 few protestants remained in the army; protestant judges were replaced with catholics; and the Catholic Church was reorganised, with money from vacant anglican benefices being used for its benefit. The rearmament of the catholic Irish recalled for Englishmen their rising in 1641.

The issue of dispensations from the Test Act was all very well, but would not guarantee the permanent re-establishment of catholicism in England. At the end of 1686 and in early 1687 James began personal interviews with office-holders, peers and MPs to discover their attitude towards the repeal of the Test Acts and penal laws. They confirmed his impression of tory hostility to his proposals. His attitude towards the Church cooled further. When in March 1687 the president of

Magdalen College, Oxford, died James requested that its fellows elect a catholic convert as his replacement. When they refused and appointed someone else, James imposed another candidate, Samuel Parker, Bishop of Oxford – an anglican, but the complete loyalist. The fellows refused him too. The ecclesiastical commission heard the case and deprived them all of their fellowships – taking away both their spiritual functions and their temporal emoluments. For what was essentially a spiritual court to apply secular punishments for an offence which was not against the law implied not only the power-grasping clericalism of popery, but also a careless disregard for private property. As the Church lost favour, the court began to look to the sort of alliance with dissent that Charles II had established in 1672. In April 1687, the king issued his own Declaration of Indulgence, suspending the penal laws and Test Acts against recusants and legal proceedings against all other nonconformists, and guaranteeing freedom of worship. The Declaration stated the government's intention to seek retrospective parliamentary sanction for its indulgence: but this was little consolation for tories, whose king had abandoned them and turned to their enemies; or for churchmen, for it was clear now that the Church could no longer rely on its established status for protection; or still for anyone who was concerned about the survival of parliament, for it showed that the government was still willing to make ever-wider use of the powers of dispensation that it felt it possessed.

It was a highly risky policy: abandoning those who had stood by James and the monarchy for those whom he had often in the past condemned as rebels and republicans was an extraordinary volte-face and one about which even the machiavellian Sunderland had qualms. And it was far from clear how much support the Declaration would receive from the dissenters themselves: none of the numerous addresses from nonconformists thanking the king for the Indulgence specifically acknowledged the king's power to suspend the Test Acts and penal laws, and about a third of them pointedly referred to a future parliamentary approval for the suspension. James thought nothing of the difficulties ahead. He ignored

Sunderland's objections, and brought yet more catholics into the council, including Father Petre, the jesuit. In early August he ordered a new purge of the livery companies of London: tories were rejected from the court of aldermen; in their place, his new allies, whigs and dissenters, were returned to power.

James at least had not misled his subjects in his announcement that he would try to obtain parliamentary approval for his suspension of the Test Acts and penal laws. In July he dissolved the parliament elected in 1685, as he prepared for an enormous inquest throughout the country to test the ground for their repeal in a new one. Lords lieutenant were required to question each JP or deputy lieutenant within their jurisdiction to establish whether they would support repeal either within or outside parliament, as well as to find and recommend catholics and dissenters who might be included in the commissions of the peace or lieutenancy. Lords lieutenant who failed to co-operate were removed; twelve of them were replaced with catholics. The inquiry itself was largely carried out in the three months from December 1687. Almost all of those who gave unfavourable or equivocal answers were removed from the commissions of the peace: catholics, dissenters and former exclusionists were put in instead. By the middle of 1688 few of the JPs who were in commission in 1685 remained. There was a similar and parallel regulation of town corporations, tightly controlled through a central regulating committee. Government agents were despatched to report on the composition and affection of town governments and *quo warranto* writs were issued accordingly. By the end of March 1688 more than 1200 members of town corporations had been removed and replaced, often by dissenters and former exclusionists. In April the campaign was extended, as the agents were sent once again into the provinces to test what the likely results of an election would be.

For tories, for many of the old gentry, these actions were extraordinary and outrageous. Many of the most powerful men in each shire, the knights and baronets, the old cavalier anglican gentry, were removed from local governments that they and their fathers had dominated for years. They were now to be ruled by men they regarded as papists, fanatics or men of no social consequence. But the dissenters' own response was perplexed. After so long a persecution, the freedom of the Indulgence was vastly tempting: yet coming from popish hands, it was deeply suspected. Only a few, mainly quakers and independents, gave it wholehearted support. Many were as suspicious of the tories as they were of the papists. Some, however, began to argue the need for anglicans and protestant nonconformists to unite in the face of the popish threat: 'it is plain to all mankind', wrote the presbyterian, Roger Morrice, 'that a coalition between the sober conformists and nonconformists is the only expedient that is within the reach of human prospect to save this nation'.[36] A few anglicans were beginning to feel the same: after all, a profound suspicion of popery and attachment to the law were things which united the protestant nation. Halifax's pamphlet of the late summer of 1687, *A Letter to a Dissenter,* warned nonconformists not to let the destruction of the law be the price of their toleration – 'after giving thanks for the breach of one law, you lose the right of complaining of the breach of all the rest' – and offered the hope of some form of comprehension or toleration in agreement with the Church. If English protestants stayed firm and united, he argued, they could sit out the reign of James II, confident in the knowledge that his heir, Princess Mary, and her husband, William of Orange, were firmly and unshakeably protestant.[37]

Over the water, William had made precisely the same calculation. Mary's eventual succession guaranteed the impermanence of James's plans to re-establish catholicism, and that he (William) would himself ultimately be in a position to influence English foreign policy. As Louis XIV's gradual encroachments in Germany threatened the resumption of European war, the English alliance was ever more important to him. But with the dismissal of Halifax and Rochester, his only real supporters at the English court, it seemed to be slipping out of his hands. James's suspicion of William's involvement with the radical enemies of his regime had never been entirely allayed; he was undoubtedly perplexed by the need to secure William's co-operation in his plans to repeal the Test Acts and penal laws, and William began to suspect that Mary might herself be excluded from the throne. In a series of informal contacts in late 1686 and 1687 the two tried to reassure each other, but at the same time William strengthened his contacts with many of the English nobility. Several asked him to take a much more active role in English politics; some even suggested his military intervention. The publication in early 1688 of a defiant account of William's position on the religious question written by his political associate Gaspar Fagel, grand pensionary of the state of Holland, which accepted toleration and the repeal of the penal laws but stood by the Test Acts, irritated James further. In March 1688 the king ordered the return to England of the English soldiers serving in the Dutch army.

The gathering European diplomatic crisis pressed William to action. The Truce of Ratisbon in 1684 had confirmed, for the moment, Louis's encroachments in Germany since 1678. Yet the continuance of his power in the area depended crucially on a complex concurrence of circumstances. As long as the Emperor Leopold I remained preoccupied with the Turks on his eastern borders, as long as England remained unwilling to intervene, as long as Louis XIV's money and diplomacy could prevent an anti-French coalition in Germany, it was secure. But from 1683, Leopold began to win a series of victories in the East, by 1688 pushing the Turks back beyond Belgrade, and several German states joined him in forming an anti-French coalition, the League of Augsburg in 1686. Although the League failed to hold together long, it did suggest a growing willingness to confront French power. The will to resist Louis was growing in the Netherlands, as well, as the Dutch began to fear that James's decision to recall English troops from the Netherlands heralded an Anglo-French alliance, such as that which had almost destroyed the republic in 1672, as their fears were reinforced by the stories of French religious persecution brought by escaping Huguenots, and as the French stepped up their commercial campaign of discriminatory tariffs against Dutch goods and services. With French influence apparently on the wane, an opportunity to test its effectiveness emerged. The Archbishop-Elector Max-Henry of Cologne, a client of Louis XIV, governed most of the Rhineland: in early 1688 he was dying, and the struggle over the election of his successor would be a vital one if Louis was to maintain his control in Western Germany.

In England, serious opposition to James was growing quickly. The results of the inquiry in April by the government's election agents showed the problems with the policy of seeking support from the dissenters: it was clear that there were few more of them than there were of anglicans who were prepared to work for the repeal of the Tests and penal laws. There was evidence, too, that both anglicans and dissenters were beginning to recognise the need for co-operation. In the same month James reissued his Declaration of Indulgence and a week later ordered that it be read in all anglican churches. The anglican clergy, given a focus of opposition, decided to exploit it, and remarkably, through informal contacts of senior churchmen and prominent dissenters, they secured the non-conformists' understanding and support. In a petition which seven of the bishops, headed by Archbishop Sancroft, drew up and presented to the king on 18 May, they requested the rescission of the order, and claimed the illegality of the Declaration. The king was furious in their presence, calling the petition 'a standard of rebellion'.[38] On 8 June, the bishops were arrested: on 29 June they were put on trial for seditious libel amid an atmosphere of enormous excitement and amazement. Even before the trial the bishops had acquired the aura of martyrs for the protestant cause; when they were acquitted there was uproarious popular rejoicing in the City, so much so that the Dutch ambassadors expected an almost spontaneous rebellion.

The crisis for English protestantism had indeed already arrived. A few days after the bishops' arrest, the English catholics were blessed with what seemed like a miracle. When the pregnancy of James's queen, Mary, had been confirmed in November 1687, the chances that she would produce a son to supplant Princess Mary as heir to the throne seemed remote:

none of her several previous children had lived. But now, to catholic delight and protestant horror, she was delivered of a son.

Since early 1688 the pressure of English dissidents on William to intervene in English politics had become intense: why he finally accepted is uncertain. Undoubtedly, by May, when he cautiously agreed to an armed landing, he was deeply worried about the possibility of either a catholic coup or a republican rebellion in England, neither of which would be of much use to him. The birth of the queen's child, suspected by many protestants to be supposititious – it seemed too convenient, too perfectly timed, and too improbable to be genuinely hers – confirmed his decision. To prevent his intervention being imputed an invasion, he demanded from his English correspondents a written invitation from leading English politicians. Few of the politically prominent nobility, however, were willing to make that sort of commitment, one that could easily be construed as treasonable. The Earl of Danby, the earls of Devonshire and Shrewsbury, besides the Bishop of London and a few of William's English allies had to suffice: the invitation was drawn up and sent to William on the night of the bishops' acquittal.

With great secrecy, and a rather adept campaign of disinformation, William set about collecting together and strengthening the Dutch forces. The fleet was already being expanded, and William assembled an army of between 14,000 and 15,000. All this was naturally noticed, but it was unclear what its purpose was. One theory was that William intended to oppose Louis XIV's anticipated military intervention in the Cologne election, although the possibility of an invasion of England was not ignored. The government strengthened the coastal defences, although it politely turned down two offers of French military help, not wishing to make any move which William might interpret as hostile. It was not, however, until mid-August that the government possessed any firm information that William's preparations were aimed at England. A few days later French troops marched towards the Rhine: in early September they occupied the Rhineland. Louis, taking the view that this would mean that William's attention would be too occupied in Germany to mount an invasion on England, committed his naval forces to the Mediterranean. But William had no intention of dropping his plans. Having obtained the full approval of the states-general on 30 September, he published a declaration announcing his intention to come to England to oversee a free election, and attacking James's ministers for the illegalities of the last four years.

The English government was sent into a frenzy of activity. Despite the riskiness of William's enterprise, shipping troops across the Channel in the teeth of the autumn gales and the Royal Navy, to face an English army with a considerable numerical superiority, ministers were aware of their complete lack of domestic support, and alarmed by the fact that they could no longer count on French military aid. The government dropped its plans for the election prepared for over the last year; instead, it promised a free election, and issued a declaration guaranteeing the rights and privileges of the established Church, and asking only for a universal toleration. It began to restore to the commissions of the peace and lieutenancy all those who had been removed over the last twelve months; the ecclesiastical commission was dissolved and the fellows of Magdalen restored; the changes to London's charter were rescinded, and in mid-October all the proceedings against all other charters since 1679 were annulled. On Sunderland's insistence, the government dropped plans for pre-emptive arrests of the English conspirators, and it began discussions with the bishops and eminent tories. It made all the military preparations it could, rapidly expanding the army, and bringing Irish and Scottish troops into England. All the available soldiers were concentrated around London. It soon became clear that James would need to put his faith in the military: the government's concessions to protestant opinion were too obviously forced to be seen as anything but insincere and cynical. As Sunderland grew more and more nervous for the future, James dismissed him.

William sailed on 19 October, but was driven back by heavy seas. It was almost two weeks before the wind would allow him to try again; when he did, on 1 November, it blew his fleet down the Channel as it blocked the English navy in its anchorages in the Thames. On 5 November he landed, unopposed, in Torbay. He was at first alarmed by the slowness with which the local gentry came in to support him, and by the meagre response in other parts of the country. But as the English army massed at Salisbury Plain to oppose him, a trickle of defecting officers began to arrive at his camp; as he moved east, they grew in number and importance, including many of the most able young senior commanders. On 20–22 November the risings by Danby and Lord Delamere planned in the North and the West Midlands to coincide with the landing, finally occurred. Some local gentry started to show their support for the prince. Even James's family went over: his nephew, the Duke of Grafton, and his son-in-law, Prince George of Denmark, joined William and worst of all, his daughter, Princess Anne, abandoned her father. As the Dutch advanced, James's army slowly disintegrated: the king himself was paralysed, not knowing whom to trust. Only two days after William left Exeter, James accepted the advice of his senior commanders – some of them in the conspiracy themselves – to retreat.

The king's return to London ended the brief military phase of the revolution. Back at Whitehall, he discussed the situation with a council of peers; at their instance he announced that parliament would open on 15 January and sent commissioners to negotiate with William, now at Hungerford. James's military impotence had left William in a gratifyingly strong but awkward position. He had come to England ostensibly simply to ensure a free parliament, and much of the local support that he received was based on that premiss; the whigs, however, who were strong among his advisers, wanted him to go further, and himself take the throne. It was the king who solved his dilemma. Progressively demoralised by the desertions and by the news of the whigs in William's entourage, James fled from Whitehall, sending his wife and son before him, to France. William was left as the only effective authority in the country. But James's escape was bungled: a few days after he left Whitehall, he was seized near the coast by some seamen, and the tories in the assembly of peers that had assumed provisional government in London during his absence brought him back to Whitehall. But despite the pleas of loyalists, James was in no mood to stay, and William's coldness confirmed his decision to leave. Two days before Christmas he slipped away, unmolested by his Dutch guards: a couple of days later he was in France.

William's victory was an astonishing achievement: he was undisputedly in effective control of the country he had so dangerously invaded a month before. His position was, however, an ambiguous one. What position did he hold? Was he king or conqueror? Since James's flight, tory loyalism had revived, exacerbated by the prince's less than magnanimous treatment of his father-in-law. When an assembly of peers was summoned by William to discuss the implications of the king's departure, it was riven by disputes between whiggish Williamites and tory loyalists. William turned instead to a new parliament, the Convention, which was elected hastily in January and met on the 22nd. For a week, whigs and tories argued over how James's departure was to be interpreted, and whether parliament might declare who was king. But the arguments over who should rule the country had given way to arguments about how to make William's coup acceptable in terms of law: for it was clear that few wished now to exchange William as ruler for anyone else, and the anxiety of almost all concerned to avoid bloodshed and civil war generated irresistible pressure for a rapid settlement. Most conservatives were more anxious to preserve the continuity of government and the rule of law than hereditary government or royal power for their own sake. Eventually a formula was found that most could accept: on 6 February parliament voted that the throne was vacant by reason of James's abdication, and that, consequently, William and Mary were joint sovereigns.

Whether William had ever intended to achieve so much is probably unknowable. Many of William's contemporaries, including some of his friends, thought he did; among his advisers in 1688 were many whigs who even in the early 1680s had been recommending William as a suitable replacement for an excluded James. In the end, however, William's expedition had not been the result of deeply laid plans; it had rather been provoked by fears of catholic plots to prevent his wife succeeding to the throne, and the imminence of European war. That William had succeeded so completely – more, perhaps, than he had hoped for when he sailed – had been due in large part to a precarious combination of conspiracy and sheer nerve. The conspiracy in the army was crucial. Many of its principal officers had long had close professional contacts with the Dutch. When in June 1688 it seemed likely that James was planning a purge of army officers similar to that he had undertaken in Ireland, many career soldiers began to discuss defection. The conspiracy riddled the senior ranks of the army: many of its colonels, among them James's closest protégés, were involved. The effect of their loss on the army itself, when it came, was perhaps not quite as great as it was on James. The desertion of some of the soldiers to whom he had devoted his own loyalty was devastating to his morale. James's irresolution in late November and early December ultimately lost him everything: even when tories pointed out to him how his presence in England would revive loyalist support, James, distrustful of betrayal, full of a paranoid fear of republicans and whigs, and frightened of the ignominious fate that befell his father, insisted on leaving.

There was little obvious reason for William to thank the English gentry. They had not opposed him, but they had done little to help him either. The risings of Lord Delamere in Cheshire and of the Earl of Devonshire in Derbyshire attracted little support among the greater gentry – even those that had supported exclusion. Such support as they received tended to come largely from the minor gentry, and often from among their younger sons. Some of greater social standing joined the risings later, such as the whig Earl of Manchester, or the Earl of Northampton, the brother of Bishop Compton. One reason for their early reluctance was doubtless the obvious and intimidating power of James's army. Another was the distaste, even religious horror, in which anglican royalists held rebellion. Even those who did join William stressed that their purpose was merely to force a new parliament, not to depose the king, and by the end of December many were horrified by the turn of events: 'I can take God to witness', wrote Danby's son after the Revolution, 'I had not a thought when I engaged in it (and I am sure my father neither) that the Prince of Orange's landing would end in deposing the king.'[39] Many others equally recoiled from political violence. Even the former whig activist, Thomas Papillon, admitted in 1688 that he wished to live 'in peace without giving offence to those that God hath set in authority over us. . . . I am resolved not to intermeddle with any affairs of state, or to converse with any that are obnoxious to the government.'[40] Rebellion could never be limited enough simply to redress a grievance; it would always overturn law and dissolve society.

Even so, William had been widely welcomed as the deliverer of the nation from popery and arbitrary government, and before his flight scarcely anyone had actually lifted a finger in the king's defence. James's assault on the traditional institutions of English government and society had profoundly alienated those who traditionally had managed them. He had turned upside down old assumptions about the way in which the country should be run, chasing national and local grandees from what they regarded as their rightful places in the privy council, the House of Commons, and the justices' benches and the commissions of lieutenancy. The anglican royalist ascendancy was destroyed in 1687 and 1688; the ascendancy of the aristocracy and greater gentry seemed likely to follow it.

Yet James's policies had struck not simply at the gentry's power, but at the shibboleths of an entire nation. The protestant religion, property and the law seemed all to be at risk from this restless tyrant. It was true that James had done nothing for which he could not find a legal justification, for the law held enough gaps and ambiguities to allow genuine disagreement on many matters which concerned royal power. But the gaps and ambiguities had in the past been filled with or interpreted by convention, and it was clear enough that if

James could argue that he was still standing by the letter of the law, his subjects might retort that he had comprehensively trampled on its spirit, at least as they understood it. The behaviour of his army and his ecclesiastical authorities gave no one confidence in the security of their property from an autocratic government, and James's recent treatment of the Church and its bishops had scarcely proved that the Church was safe in his hands. If his subjects did not rally to defend him, James had only himself to blame: for he had given none of them any reason to.

6

CONCLUSION

'Let [the king] come in, and call a parliament of the greatest cavaliers in England, so they be men of estates, and let them sit but 7 years, and they will all turn Commonwealth's men', prophesied James Harrington in early 1660.[1] Within seven years, indeed, the Restoration government was in an acute political crisis; after three decades of political conflict it succumbed, almost without a fight, to Prince William and his Dutch troops. Had the attempt to reconstruct the pre-Civil War polity been (as both Harrington and Hobbes, for different reasons, would have thought) fundamentally misconceived? Historians in the past have believed so: the Civil War both demonstrated the inadequacy of England's antique system of government, and pushed it further into obsolescence; no longer could it accommodate the aspirations of a politically mature people, and no longer could it deliver the stability they craved.

Political stability is an elusive concept, as difficult to define as it may be to create. One definition might be a willingness to resolve conflicts within the established political and legal systems and conventions. In that sense, at least, England seemed stable enough. For all the fears they aroused, radical terrorism and political violence were not very common in Restoration England. Outlandish religious sects, such as the quakers, for the most part carried out their campaign for freedom of conscience by exploiting the law, rather than trying to pull it down; and even the government usually sought the

143

freedom it wanted within the established constitutional framework rather than outside it. Above all, the powerful political elite saw the antiquity of England's system of government as her blessing, not her curse, and saw their power dependent not on expanding their own role, but on preserving the close links between themselves and the Crown that it guaranteed.

Another definition, though, might depend on the extent to which a country's various elements were prepared to place trust in one another. It was perhaps the more essential point for England's constitutional system, which depended heavily on a large degree of mutual trust and co-operation: of parliament and government, of Crown and political elite. Her constitution and her law were regarded with exaggerated reverence: what was lacking was the belief that the other parties to it shared that reverence. 'The great happiness of any government rests principally in this', wrote the great Restoration lawyer, Sir Matthew Hale, commenting on Hobbes's *Dialogue between a Philosopher and a Student of the Common-Laws of England*: 'namely the mutual confidence that the governors have in the people as to point of duty and obedience and that the governed have in their governors as to point of protection.' 'The first breach that happens in this golden knot as by miserable experience we have learned', he went on, comes

> when insinuations of diffidence and distrust and jealousies are secretly nourished or openly made, and most certainly there is not any one more mischievous and pernicious root of jealousies and diffidences than to tell the world that the prince is bound to keep none of the laws that he or his ancestors have by the advice of his great council established [and] that he may repeal them when he sees cause. That all his subjects' properties depend upon his pleasure. That there is no law so strictly and prudently penned for the securing of his subjects' liberties and properties, but they intrinsically have this condition implied, though not expressed: that when he judgeth it fit he may suspend or abrogate them.[2]

The origins of the political conflicts of Restoration England lay not so much in the disjunction between political and economic power, or in parliament's ambitions for a greater role in government, but in the sheer weight of the uncertainties and anxieties on all sides. Fears that the government's desire for the reassurance of strength might bring it to disregard the country's traditions of self-government; that individual ministers were too corrupt to care about law or constitutional convention; that the gentry were being edged out of political and economic influence by a mixture of corruption and financial decline; and the government's own fears of radical violence and parliamentary assertiveness, dominated Restoration politics.

James II's determined effort to revive catholicism caused him to trample over all these English political sensibilities. Law, social hierarchy and property all seemed irrelevant in the desperate pursuit of a single ambition. The monarchy that in 1660 had been restored in order to recreate an ordered, predictable world (if one had ever existed) had become as unpredictable and as dangerous as the Rump Parliament and its army. In his popery lay the epitome of disorder and instability. Its bloody ruthlessness, its single-minded determination, its fundamental irrationality, represented all of the insecurity that the country had tried to escape. It was, England believed, a cancer which lay at her heart, corrupting her from within.

It was not England's only religious cancer, of course, for anglican royalists and churchmen regarded protestant dissent as an infection which, if not severely treated, might spread to the whole nation. Unity in religion, wrote the lawyer Sir Robert Pointz, was 'the chiefest pillar that upholdeth human society, and obedience to supreme authority, which cannot stand after religion is fallen'.[3] Dissent might be as dangerous to political stability as illegality or disregard of the constitution. Indeed the Church 'by law established' was, in effect, part of the constitution: to alter its status and privileges was fundamentally to alter the law. The way in which attempts to introduce toleration tried to skirt around the law with suspensions and dispensations, simply encouraged the association of religious pluralism with violation of law. To the deeply conservative gentry of Restoration England it was better to accept anglican royalists' arguments and dismiss demands to liberalise the Church than to risk the unpredictable effects of change.

It was James who may have broken the power of anglican arguments against protestant dissent. As fears of popery grew, from the early 1670s, fear of protestant nonconformity declined. It was not dead, and proved easy enough to revive in the early 1680s. But with the revelation of the catholic king's determination to promote his religion, the general resistance to nonconformity all but collapsed, and those committed anglicans who had fought so long and so hard to prevent either the comprehension or the toleration of dissent were left whistling in the dark. Sir John Reresby, a Yorkshire tory, observed that by 1687 'most men were now convinced that liberty of conscience was a thing of advantage to the nation, as it might be settled with due regard to the rights and privileges of the Church of England'.[4] But dissent itself had changed. Decades of frustration and moments of temptation to separatism had brought many to change their minds about the virtues of a single national church. The numbers of presbyterians who were still committed to securing comprehension within the Church of England had shrunk: presbyterians, wrote one anglican minister in 1689, 'are but few now, most of them being run into Independency'.[5] In 1689 clerical opposition prevented an attempt to introduce comprehension, but the Toleration Act passed in its stead confirmed the dissenters' drift to separation.[6]

The Revolution brought a transformation, too, of England's position in international politics. Within three months of William and Mary's joint accession, William had declared war on France. For almost a quarter-of-a-century henceforward, England's forces were to be closely involved in fighting continental wars against her. William dragged the country into the firm international commitment that she had never found under Restoration governments. Her haphazard alliances were swept away and replaced by a more certain alignment. And her wars transformed her politics as well. The massive financial requirements of an enormous continental war were, over the next decade, as drastically to affect the relationship of government and parliament as had Charles II's wars. This time, however, a developing financial system, matched with an enormous expansion of the permanent armed forces, was to revolutionise it. The Revolution did not banish completely the fears and anxieties which had dominated Restoration politics; indeed, in some ways it embittered them. Yet ultimately, it was to permit the emergence of a parliamentary system which could accommodate political distrust by making changes of government routine.

Like the change in religious attitudes, these transformations, considerable though they may have been, had nevertheless been foreshadowed during the Restoration. The pressure on England's rulers to become part of a new international alliance against Louis XIV had been growing since the mid-1660s; for twenty years isolated diplomats had worked, later on with Prince William of Orange, to try to create a new power bloc to resist France. Not until the mid-1680s did they begin to succeed, and James's removal took away the last obstacle to its completion. But in other ways, England had laid in the Restoration the foundation of her international power. The two wars against the Dutch – particularly that of 1672–4 – had begun to sap the commercial strength of her greatest mercantile rival, even though they had also harmed England's post-Civil War recovery; and the boom in England's trade in the later 1670s and 1680s was the first sign of how she might come to benefit from her eighteenth-century trading power. Even one of the bases of the new political system – party government – was at least hinted at in the precocious sophistication that politicians achieved at the height of the 'Exclusion Crisis' in the early 1680s.

England's recovery from civil war was a long and painful process. The war's violence and illegality haunted Restoration politics, as the country sought to find again the stability that (her people believed) she had enjoyed for so long before the Civil War. The themes of Restoration politics mirrored those of the Civil War: the threat of popery and protestant dissent, the fear of arbitrary government and anarchy, the concern about corruption. Yet it would be wrong to see the restored monarchy as a weak and feeble regime, little better than its Interregnum predecessors, barely managing to enforce its will any more effectively than they. In many ways – in its small army, in its growing revenues, and in the extent to which central government was beginning to intervene in local affairs – Charles II and James II in the 1680s were more powerful than any of their ancestors: and over their immediate predecessors, they possessed the enormous advantage of legitimacy.[7] It was clear that the Restoration failed fully to solve the problems which had caused the Civil War and perplexed English politics since the Reformation and before it: no simple change of government, perhaps, could do as much. Nor did it instantly produce complete political stability. It would be another century before English politicians could fling Bishop Bossuet's words back across the Channel and claim that France's despotism provided a less stable government than their own constitutional monarchy. But the reassertion of legitimate government was perhaps the first step in the creation of stability, and one that they were careful to remember in 1689, as they decided how to legalise William's conquest. And while it might take years and subtle shifts in power between Crown and parliament to resolve the mutual distrust of people and government, in their determination to prevent political conflict from disturbing conventions of law and society the political leaders of England exemplified the underlying forces that might lead towards a more fundamental stability.

Notes

1. INTRODUCTION

1. *The diurnal of Thomas Rugge, 1659–1661*, ed. W. L. Sachse (Camden Society, 3rd series, XCI, 1961), p. 87; *The Life of Edward Hyde, Earl of Clarendon* (Oxford, 1857), 2 vols, I, 268.
2. J. B. Bossuet, *Oraison Funèbre de Henriette de France*, in Bossuet, *Oraisons Funèbres*, ed. J. Truchet (Paris, 1961), pp. 125–6.
3. Thomas Otway, *Venice Preserv'd*, ed. M. Kelsall (London, 1969), II, iii, 20–1.
4. Bodleian Library, Tanner MS 239, fol. 53.
5. M. G. Davies, 'Country gentry and falling rents in the 1660s and 1670s', *Midland History*, IV (1977–8), 95, n. 49.
6. *The Political Works of James Harrington*, ed. J. G. A. Pocock (Cambridge, 1977), 'The preliminaries', of *Oceana*.
7. Thomas Hobbes, *Leviathan*, ed. C. B. Macpherson (Harmondsworth, 1968).
8. Joan Thirsk, *The Agricultural History of England and Wales*, V, i (Cambridge, 1984), xix–xxvii, xxviii.
9. M. G. Davies, 'Country gentry and falling rents', p. 88.
10. Quoted by B. Manning, *The English People and the English Revolution* (Harmondsworth, 1978), p. 215.
11. Anthony Fletcher, *The Reform of the Provinces: the government of Stuart England* (London, 1986), pp. 221–7.
12. Alexander Brome, *Songs and Poems* (London, 1668), p. 323.
13. Edward Waterhouse, *The Gentleman's Monitor* (London, 1665).
14. Samuel Parker, *A Discourse of Ecclesiastical Polity* (London, 1669), p. vi.
15. *John Locke: Two tracts on government*, ed. P. Abrams (Cambridge, 1967), p. 211.
16. R. Macgillivray, *Restoration Historians and the English Civil War* (The Hague, 1974), pp. 227–8.

17. Sir Robert Pointz, *A vindication of monarchy* (London, 1661), p. 47.

18. *The correspondence of Bishop Brian Duppa and Sir Justinian Isham, 1650–1660*, ed. Sir Gyles Isham, Publications of the Northamptonshire Record Society, XVII (1951), p. 186.

19. *The Life of Edward Hyde, Earl of Clarendon*, (2 vols, Oxford 1857), I, 273–4.

2. CONFLICTS OF POWER

1. Public Record Office, SP 29/81/94 (Earl of Peterborough, October 1663); for the contradictions of Restoration royalism, see James Daly, 'The idea of absolute monarchy in seventeenth-century England', *Historical Journal* xxi (1978), 239 ff.

2. *The Life of Edward Hyde, Earl of Clarendon*, II, 347.

3. Bodleian Library, Carte MS 46, fol. 64.

4. Andrew Browning, *Thomas Osborne, Earl of Danby and Duke of Leeds 1632–1712* (3 vols, Glasgow, 1944–51), I, 338.

5. C. C. Weston and J. R. Greenberg, *Subjects and Sovereigns: the grand controversy over legal sovereignty in Stuart England* (Cambridge, 1981), ch. 6.

6. For criticism of Weston and Greenberg on 'co-ordination', see J. P. Sommerville, *Politics and Ideology in England, 1603–1640* (London, 1986), p. 175.

7. *The genuine remains in verse and prose of Mr Samuel Butler*, ed. R. Thyer (2 vols, London, 1759), I, 419–20.

8. Sir Roger Twysden, *Certain considerations upon the government of England*, ed. J. M. Kemble, Camden Society, old series, XLV (1849), p. 172.

9. Bodleian Library, Tanner MSS 239, fol. 57v.

10. John Miller, 'The Restoration Monarchy', in *The restored monarchy, 1660–1688*, ed. J. R. Jones (London, 1979); J. R. Jones, *Charles II: royal politician* (London, 1987), pp. 187–90.

11. John Miller, *James II: a study in kingship* (Hove, 1978).

12. R. L. Greaves, *The Radical Underground in Britain, 1660–3* (New York, 1986); Jonathan Scott, *Algernon Sidney and the English Republic 1623–1677* (Cambridge, 1988), pp. 151 ff.

13. L. von Ranke, *A history of England, principally in the seventeenth century* (6 vols, Oxford, 1875), III, 337.

14. *The Life of Edward Hyde, Earl of Clarendon*, I, 615; II, 226.

15. *The parliamentary history of England, from the earliest period to 1803*, ed. W. Cobbett and J. Wright (36 vols, London, 1806–20), IV, 185.

16. C. D. Chandaman, *The English Public Revenue, 1660–1688* (Oxford, 1975); Paul Seaward, *The Cavalier Parliament and the*

Reconstruction of the Old Regime, 1661–1667 (Cambridge, 1989), ch. 5, and pp. 237–41; for the 'Stop of the Exchequer', see H. Roseveare, *The Treasury, 1660–1870: the foundations of control* (London, 1973), ch. 1.

17. Seaward, *Cavalier Parliament*, ch. 5.
18. Chandaman, *English Public Revenue*, ch. 4; cf. e.g. Browning, *Danby*, I, 186–90.
19. Bodleian Library, Carte MSS 46, fol. 516, 30 July 1667.
20. *Poems on Affairs of State*, ed. G. De F. Lord (6 vols, New Haven, 1963–), I, 141.
21. Roseveare, *The Treasury*, pp. 51–6.
22. Weston and Greenberg, *Subjects and Sovereigns*, pp. 153–6; 13 Car. II, c. 6.
23. Seaward, *Cavalier Parliament*, pp. 135–40.
24. Ibid., pp. 94–9, 297–301.
25. See, for example, ibid., pp. 217–32.
26. Andrew Marvell, *An account of the growth of popery and arbitrary government in England* ([London], 1677), p. 80.
27. Seaward, *Cavalier Parliament*, pp. 79–92, 225–6; Dennis Witcombe, *Charles II and the Cavalier House of Commons, 1663–1674* (Manchester, 1966), p. 49; *The Alarum* is printed in *English Historical Documents, 1660–1714*, ed. Andrew Browning (London, 1953), pp. 233–6.
28. Browning, *Danby*, I, 191–3; cf. Andrew Browning, 'Parties and party organisation in the reign of Charles II', *Transactions of the Royal Historical Society*, 4th series, XXX (1948), 21–36.
29. S. K. Roberts, *Recovery and Restoration in an English County: Devon local administration, 1649–70* (Exeter, 1985), p. 218.
30. Seaward, *Cavalier Parliament*, pp. 134–7.
31. L. J. Glassey, *Politics and the Appointment of Justices of the Peace, 1675–1720* (Oxford, 1979), ch. 2; cf. C. G. F. Forster, 'Government in provincial England under the later Stuarts', *Transactions of the Royal Historical Society*, 5th series, XXXIII (1983), 29–48.
32. Public Record Office, SP 29/1/81.
33. *Poems and Fables of John Dryden*, ed. J. Kinsley (Oxford, 1970), 'Astrea Redux', II. 46–7; Bristol University Library, DM 155/133 (Henry Bull, Dec. 1674).
34. Anchitel Grey, *Debates in the House of Commons from the year 1667 to the year 1694* (10 vols, London, 1763), I, 274, cf. 352; cf. Seaward, *Cavalier Parliament*, p. 260.
35. *The Diary of Samuel Pepys*, ed. R. Latham and W. Matthews (11 vols, London, 1970–83), VIII, 324; cf. *The Life of Edward Hyde, Earl of Clarendon*, II, 469.
36. R. L'Estrange, *A memento: directed to all those that truly reverence the memory of King Charles the martyr* (London, 1662), p. 84.

37. Anthony Fletcher, *Reform in the Provinces: the government of Stuart England* (London, 1986) pp. 324–32; Seaward, *Cavalier Parliament*, pp. 141–51.

38. J. Childs, *The Army of Charles II* (London, 1976), pp. 87–8, 196–209; A. Coleby, 'Military-civilian relations on the Solent, 1651–89', *Historical Journal*, XXIX (1986), 949–61.

39. Grey, *Debates*, II, 216.

40. Ibid., II, 221.

41. Seaward, *Cavalier Parliament*, p. 307; C. H. Hartmann, *Charles II and Madame* (London, 1934), pp. 279–80.

42. Browning, *Danby*, II, 68–9.

43. A. M. Coleby, *Central Government and the Localities: Hampshire 1649–89* (Cambridge, 1987), pp. 90–1; cf. Roberts, *Recovery and Restoration in an English County*, pp. 146–67.

44. J. R. Jones, 'The first whig party in Norfolk', *Durham University Journal*, XLVI (1953), 13–21; see also L. J. Glassey, *Politics and the Appointment of Justices of the Peace* (Oxford, 1980), pp. 32–8.

45. See the accounts of J. H. Sacret, 'The Restoration government and municipal corporations', *English Historical Review*, XLV (1930), 232–59; J. Miller, 'The Crown and the borough charters in the reign of Charles II', *English Historical Review*, C (1985), 53–84; Seaward, *Cavalier Parliament*, pp. 151–7.

46. R. Hutton, *The Restoration: a political and religious history of England and Wales, 1658–1667* (Oxford, 1985), p. 135; British Library, Loan MS 29/51; Seaward, *Cavalier Parliament*, pp. 52–6.

47. Seaward, *Cavalier Parliament*, pp. 196–209.

48. R. L'Estrange, *A Caveat to the Cavaliers* (London, 1661), p. 25.

49. Public Record Office, SP 29/269/100 (December 1669).

50. Browning, *Danby*, III, 4–5.

3. CONFLICTS OF CONSCIENCE

1. Quoted by Mark Goldie, 'Sir Peter Pett, sceptical toryism, and the science of toleration in the 1680s', *Persecution and Toleration*, Studies in Church History, XXI (1984), p. 265.

2. *Reliquiae Baxterianae: or Mr Richard Baxter's narrative of the most memorable passages of his life and times*, ed. M. Sylvester (London, 1696), part 1, p. 31.

3. Samuel Butler, *Hudibras*, ed. J. Wilders (Oxford, 1967), I, i, 1–8.

4. Barry Reay, 'The quakers, 1659, and the Restoration of the monarchy', *History*, LXIII (1978), 193–213; see J. F. Macgregor and B. Reay, *Radical Religion in the English Revolution* (Oxford, 1984), ch. 6.

5. J. S. Morrill, 'The Church in England, 1642–1649', in *Reactions to the English Civil War, 1642–9*, ed. J. S. Morrill (London, 1982), pp. 89–114.

6. *The Diary of John Milward*, ed. C. Robbins (Cambridge, 1938), p. 221; Grey, *Debates*, II, 134; J. Spurr, 'Latitudinarians and the Restoration Church', *Historical Journal*, XXXI (1988), 78–82.

7. R. S. Bosher, *The Making of the Restoration Settlement: the influence of the Laudians* (Westminster, 1951), ch. 1; R. A. Beddard, 'The Restoration Church', in *The Restored Monarchy*, ed. J. R. Jones, pp. 156–9; Seaward, *Cavalier Parliament*, pp. 62–7.

8. *The Diary of John Milward*, p. 219.

9. *The Diary of Samuel Pepys*, IX, 60.

10. For Southampton's anglican royalism, see Lois Schwoerer, *Lady Rachel Russell: 'one of the best of women'* (Baltimore, 1988), ch. 1.

11. *The Complete Works of George Savile, First Marquess of Halifax*, ed. W. Raleigh (Oxford, 1912), p. 187; Hutton, *The Restoration*, p. 200.

12. Seaward, *Cavalier Parliament*, pp. 67–70, 162–95.

13. Ibid., pp. 318–19; R. Thomas, 'Comprehension and indulgence', in *From Uniformity to Unity, 1662–1962*, ed. O. Chadwick and G. F. Nuttall (London, 1962) pp. 189–253; J. Spurr, 'The Church of England, comprehension, and the 1689 Toleration Act', *English Historical Review*, CIV (1989), 927–46.

14. Tim Harris, 'The Bawdy House Riots of 1668', *Historical Journal*, XXIX (1986), 537–56; cf. Richard Ashcraft, *Revolutionary Politics and Locke's 'Two Treatises of Government'* (Princeton, 1986), ch. 2.

15. See the discussion of the dispensation issue in early Stuart England in Sommerville, *Politics and Ideology in England*, pp. 204–7.

16. Grey, *Debates*, II, 92.

17. Browning, *Danby*, I, 146 n. 1.

18. *Poems on affairs of state*, I, 318, 'An answer to the Geneva ballad'.

19. I. M. Green, *The Re-establishment of the Church of England, 1660–1663* (Oxford, 1978), pp. 165–77; J. Spurr, 'Latitudinarians and the Restoration Church', pp. 68–77; R. Clark, 'Why was the re-establishment of the Church of England possible?', *Midland History*, VIII (1983).

20. P. Jenkins, *The Making of a Ruling Class: the Glamorganshire gentry, 1640–1790* (Cambridge, 1983), p. 118; A. Fletcher, 'The enforcement of the Conventicle Acts, 1664–1679', in *Persecution and Toleration*, Studies in Church History, XXI (1984), 238–9.

21. See, for example, Jonathan Barry, 'The politics of religion in Restoration Bristol', in *The Politics of Religion in Restoration England, 1660–1688*, ed. T. Harris, M. Goldie and P. Seaward (Oxford, 1990), pp. 168–71.

22. Fletcher, 'The enforcement of the Conventicle Acts', p. 243.
23. Seaward, *Cavalier Parliament*, p. 61.
24. *The Compton Census of 1676*, ed. Anne Whiteman, British Academy Records of Social and Economic history, new series vol. X (Oxford, 1986), introduction.
25. See J. H. Pruett, *The Parish Clergy under the later Stuarts: the Leicestershire experience* (Urbana, Illinois, 1978); Anne Whiteman, 'The episcopate of Dr Seth Ward, Bishop of Exeter and Salisbury', unpublished D.Phil thesis, University of Oxford, 1951; John Spurr, 'Anglican apologetic and the Restoration Church', unpublished D.Phil thesis, University of Oxford, 1985.
26. John Spurr, 'Virtue, religion and government: the anglican uses of providence', in *Politics of Religion in Restoration England*, ed. Harris, Goldie and Seaward, p. 36.
27. John Spurr, 'Latitudinarians and the Restoration Church', pp. 77–82.
28. Michael Hunter, *Science and Society in Restoration England* (Cambridge, 1981), ch. 7; see Spurr, 'Anglican apologetic and the Restoration Church'.
29. Robin Clifton, *The Last Popular Rebellion: the Western rising of 1685* (London, 1985), p. 57; see in general, J. Miller, *Popery and Politics in England, 1660–1688* (Cambridge, 1973).
30. Whiteman, *The Compton Census*, p. lxxvii.
31. Grey, *Debates*, IV, 188.
32. William Bedloe, *A narrative and impartial discovery of the horrid Popish Plot* (London, 1679), p. 2.
33. Bodleian Library, Carte MSS 47, fol. 127.
34. Seaward, *Cavalier Parliament*, p. 240.
35. Ibid., pp. 226–30.
36. See W. M. Lamont, *Richard Baxter and the Millenium* (London, 1979), ch. 2.
37. J. G. Simms, 'The Restoration, 1660–85', in *A New History of Ireland*, ed. T. W. Moody, F. X. Martin and F. J. Byrne, III (Oxford, 1976), 420–33; Grey, *Debates*, II, 119–20.
38. See chapter 4 below, and R. Hutton, 'The making of the secret treaty of Dover, 1668–70', *Historical Journal*, XXIX (1986), 297–318.
39. Gilbert Burnet, *History of My Own Time*, ed. O. Airy (2 vols, Oxford, 1897–1900), II, 3.
40. *Poems on affairs of state*, I, 214–15.
41. For Danby's association with the Church, see Mark Goldie, 'Danby, the bishops, and the whigs', in *The Politics of Religion in Restoration England*, ed. Harris, Goldie and Seaward, pp. 81–92; and R. A. Beddard, 'Wren's mausoleum for Charles I and the cult of the royal martyr', *Architectural History*, XXVII (1984), 36–49; and Browning, *Danby*, I, ch. 9.
42. Marvell, *An account of the growth of popery*, pp. 3, 14.

4. CONFLICTS ABROAD

1. John Locke, *Two Treatises of Government*, ed. P. Laslett (2nd edn, Cambridge, 1967), p. 427.
2. Edmund Waller, 'A panegyric to my Lord Protector, of the present greatness, and joint interest, of his Highness and this nation', in *Poems, & c., written upon several occasions* (7th edition, London, 1705), p. 366.
3. Public Record Office, PRO 31/3/109 (15/25 July 1661).
4. Keith Feiling, *British Foreign Policy, 1660–1672* (London, 1930), pp. 9, 56.
5. I am grateful to Steve Pincus for stressing this point.
6. See C. M. Andrews, *British Committees, Commissions, and Councils of Trade and Plantations, 1622–1675* (Johns Hopkins University studies in Historical and Political Science, XXVI, Baltimore, 1908).
7. See Henry Roseveare, 'Prejudice and policy: Sir George Downing as parliamentary entrepreneur', in *Enterprise and History: Essays in Honour of Charles Wilson*, ed. D. C. Coleman and P. Mathias (Cambridge, 1984), pp. 135–50.
8. Feiling, *British Foreign Policy*, p. 95.
9. Jonathan Scott, *Algernon Sidney and the English Republic* (Cambridge, 1987), pp. 215, 204–5.
10. See Simon Schama, *The Embarrassment of Riches: an interpretation of Dutch culture in the golden age* (London, 1987), pp. 257–88.
11. *The Diary of Samuel Pepys*, II, 188.
12. Quoted by K. H. D. Haley, *An English Diplomat in the Low Countries: Sir William Temple and John De Witt, 1665–72* (Oxford, 1986), p. 53.
13. F. Fox, *Great Ships: the Battlefleet of Charles II* (Greenwich, 1980), appendix II; J. R. Tanner, 'The administration of the navy from the Restoration to the Revolution', *English Historical Review*, XII (1897), 52, 701–2.
14. See, for example, J. D. Davies, 'Pepys and the Admiralty Commission of 1679–84', *Historical Research*, LXII (1989), 44–7; Seaward, *Cavalier Parliament*, pp. 237–8.
15. See R. A. Stradling, 'Spanish conspiracy in England, 1661–3', *English Historical Review*, LXXXVIII (1973); for the fullest account of Anglo-Spanish relations, see R. A. Stradling's unpublished 1968 University of Wales thesis, 'Anglo-Spanish relations, 1660–1668'.
16. Longleat House, Wiltshire, Coventry MSS 102, fol. 3ff.
17. Paul Seaward, 'The House of Commons committee of trade and the origins of the Second Anglo-Dutch War, 1664', *Historical Journal*, XXX (1987), 437–52.
18. See e.g. K. N. Chaudhuri, 'Treasure and trade balances: the East India Company's export trade, 1660–1720', *Economic History Review*, 2nd series, XXI (1968), 482, 492, 497, table 1.

19. Seaward, *Cavalier Parliament*, pp. 237–41, 303–4.
20. J. B. Wolff, *Louis XIV* (paperback edn, London, 1970), pp. 252–3; *The Diary of Samuel Pepys*, IX, 18, cf. VIII, 297–300.
21. Fox, *Great Ships*, pp. 121–3.
22. *The Diary of Samuel Pepys*, IX, 431–2, cf. 397.
23. Haley, *An English diplomat*, ch. 6.
24. Hutton, 'The making of the secret Treaty of Dover'.
25. S. B. Baxter, *William III* (London, 1966), pp. 57–85.
26. See K. H. D. Haley, *William of Orange and the English Opposition, 1672–1674* (Oxford, 1953).
27. Grey, *Debates*, II, 226.
28. Ibid., 228, 239–40.
29. C. G. A. Clay, *Economic Expansion and Social Change: England, 1500–1700* (2 vols, Cambridge, 1984), II, 154–82.
30. G. F. Zook, 'The company of Royal Adventurers of England trading into Africa, 1660–1672', *Journal of Negro History*, IV (1919); K. G. Davies, *The Royal African Company* (London, 1957).
31. K. H. D. Haley, *The first Earl of Shaftesbury* (Oxford, 1968), p. 257.
32. S. S. Webb, *The Governors-General: the English army and the definition of the Empire* (Williamsburg, 1979); and see also his *1676: the end of American independence* (Cambridge, Mass., 1985).
33. Webb, *The Governors-General*, p. 260.
34. *The Life of Edward Hyde, Earl of Clarendon*, I, 420.
35. S. Hornstein, *The Deployment of the English Navy in Peacetime, 1674–1688* (Leiden: Rijksuniversiteit te Leiden, 1985).
36. *The works of Sir William Temple, bart* (4 vols, London, 1757), II, 239.
37. M. Priestley, 'Anglo-French trade and the "unfavourable balance" controversy, 1660–1685', *Economic History Review*, 2nd series, IV (1951), 37–52.
38. Grey, *Debates*, IV, 389.
39. *Poems on affairs of state*, I, 286.

5. FROM CONFLICT TO REVOLUTION: ENGLAND IN THE 1680s

1. Roger North, *Examen, or an enquiry into the credit and veracity of a pretended complete history* (London, 1740), pp. 177–8.
2. Grey, *Debates*, VII, 51.
3. Ibid., 141.
4. Ibid., 139.
5. *The trials of William Ireland, Thomas Pickering, and John Green for conspiring the murder of the king* (London, 1678).

6. *A letter from a Gentleman in the City, to one in the country, concerning the Bill for disabling the Duke of York to inherit the imperial Crown of this Realm* (London, 1680), p. 3.

7. Grey, *Debates*, VII, 149.

8. Burnet, *History of My Own Time*, II, 220.

9. *Poems on affairs of state*, II, 375.

10. Grey, *Debates*, VII, 251–2.

11. Ibid., 419–20.

12. For the debate see Ashcraft, *Revolutionary Politics and Locke's 'Two Treatises'*, ch. 5, and Mark Goldie, 'John Locke and Restoration anglicanism', *Political Studies* XXXI (1983), 61–95.

13. See Jonathan Scott, *Algernon Sidney and the Restoration Crisis, 1678–1683* (Cambridge, forthcoming). I am grateful to Dr Scott for allowing me to see the typescript of his book before publication.

14. G. De Krey, 'London radicals and revolutionary politics, 1675–83', in *The Politics of Religion in Restoration England*, ed. Harris, Goldie and Seaward, pp. 134–62.

15. Tim Harris, *London Crowds in the Reign of Charles II* (Cambridge, 1987), pp. 100–1; D. F. Allen, 'Political clubs in Restoration London', *Historical Journal*, XIX (1976), 561–80.

16. Tim Harris, 'Was the tory reaction popular?', forthcoming in *London Journal*. I am grateful to Dr Harris for allowing me to see an early draft of his article.

17. Harris, *London Crowds in the Reign of Charles II*, p. 137.

18. *His majestie's declaration to all his loving subjects, touching the causes and reasons that moved him to dissolve the two last parliaments* (London, 1681).

19. Dryden, *Poems and Fables*, p. 228, ll. 82–7.

20. R. A. Beddard, 'The retreat on toryism: Lionel Ducket, member for Calne, and the politics of conservatism', *Wiltshire Archaeological Magazine*, LXXII/LXXIII (1980), 105–6.

21. Miller, 'The Crown and the borough charters in the reign of Charles II'.

22. Coleby, *Central Government and the Localities*, pp. 200–3.

23. Glassey, *Politics and the Appointment of Justices of the Peace*, pp. 45–62.

24. See, for example, the Kent towns quoted in C. G. Lee, '"Fanatic magistrates": religious and political conflict in three Kentish boroughs 1680–1684', forthcoming in *Historical Journal*. I am grateful to Colin Lee for allowing me to see an early draft of his article.

25. Miller, 'The Crown and the borough charters in the reign of Charles II', pp. 79–80.

26. Although cf. J. R. Jones, *Charles II: royal politician*, pp. 184–6.

27. Sir John Dalrymple, *Memoirs of Great Britain and Ireland* (3 vols, London, 1790), part I, book II, 160–1.

28. Ibid., appendix to part I, book II, 2, 4.
29. Miller, 'The Crown and the borough charters in the reign of Charles II', p. 78.
30. *The History of Parliament: the House of Commons, 1660–1690*, ed. B. D. Henning (3 vols, London, 1983), I, 27, 46–7, 56, 59.
31. *The Diary of John Evelyn*, ed. E. S. de Beer (5 vols, Oxford, 1955), IV, 434; cf. *The autobiography of Sir John Bramston*, ed. Lord Braybrooke, Camden Society, old series, XXXII (1845), p. 198.
32. D. R. Lacey, *Dissent and Parliamentary Politics in England, 1661–1689* (New Brunswick, 1969), pp. 171–2; Clifton, *The Last Popular Rebellion*, pp. 272–4.
33. *The Diary of John Evelyn*, IV, 460.
34. Grey, *Debates*, VIII, 358.
35. *The Diary of John Evelyn*, IV, 535–6.
36. Lacey, *Dissent and Parliamentary Politics*, p. 187.
37. Halifax, *Works*, p. 135.
38. Bodleian Library, Tanner MSS 28 part 1, fol. 38v.
39. *The History of Parliament*, III, 185.
40. *Memoirs of Thomas Papillon*, ed. A. F. W. Papillon (Reading, 1887), p. 261.

6. CONCLUSION

1. *'Brief lives', chiefly of contemporaries, set down by John Aubrey between the years 1669 and 1696*, ed. A. Clarke (2 vols, Oxford, 1898), I, 291.
2. 'Sir Matthew Hale on Hobbes: an unpublished manuscript', ed. F. Pollock and W. S. Holdsworth, *Law Quarterly Review*, 37 (1921), 301.
3. Sir Robert Pointz, *A vindication of monarchy*, p. 35.
4. *Memoirs of Sir John Reresby*, ed. A. Browning (Glasgow, 1935), p. 497.
5. B. L., Egerton MSS 3337, fol. 2v, quoted by John Spurr, 'The Church of England, comprehension and the 1689 Toleration Act', p. 945.
6. See in general, Spurr, 'The Church of England, comprehension and the 1689 Toleration Act'.
7. See J. R. Western, *Monarchy and Revolution: the English state in the 1680s* (London, 1972).

Bibliography

The Restoration still does not attract the sort of historiographical interest that the preceding and following periods do, but there is nevertheless a considerable amount of valuable recent work on which re-evaluations will, in time, be based. This bibliography makes no claim to exhaustiveness, but aims only to provide an introductory selection of further writings on the themes discussed in this book. W. L. Sachse, *Restoration England 1660–1689* (Cambridge: for the Conference on British Studies, 1971) is a comprehensive bibliography of works published before 1969.

Among the most accessible contemporary accounts of the Restoration political world is Gilbert Burnet's *History*, published as *Bishop Burnet's History of his Own Time* in the edition of M. J. Routh (7 vols, Oxford, 1823); there is an Everyman edition of extracts. Samuel Pepys' *Diary*, ed. R. Latham and W. Matthews (London, 1970–83, 11 vols) is as essential for the political as for the social history of the period it covers (1660–69). Some of the style of Restoration political and religious polemic can be found in Andrew Marvell's *The Rehearsall Transpros'd, and The Rehearsall Transpros'd, the second part*, ed. D. I. B. Smith (Oxford, 1971), and in his *Poems and Letters,* ed. H. M. Margoliouth (2nd edn, Oxford, 1952, 2 vols), and in Samuel Butler's *Hudibras,* ed. John Wilders (Oxford, 1967).

There are a number of general guides to the Restoration, although none has really surpassed David Ogg's *England in the Reign of Charles II* (2nd edn, Oxford, 1955, 2 vols), and *England in the Reigns of James II and William III* (Corrected edn, Oxford, 1955). J. R. Jones, *Country and Court: England 1658–1714* (London, 1978) is useful. Charles II has recently acquired a new biographer: Ronald Hutton, *Charles II, King of England, Scotland and Ireland* (Oxford, 1989); James II is described in John Miller, *James II: A Study in Kingship* (Hove, 1978). J. R. Jones, *Charles II: Royal Politician* is a selective account of Charles's political skills. The politics of the 1660s are generally discussed by Ronald Hutton, *The Restoration: a political and religious history of*

England and Wales, 1658–1667 (Oxford, 1985), and Maurice Lee, *The Cabal* (Urbana, Illinois, 1965) gives an account of the period 1667–73. Biographies, however, provide some of the best political narratives for the period: particularly K. H. D. Haley's *The First Earl of Shaftesbury* (Oxford, 1968) and Andrew Browning's *Thomas Osborne, Earl of Danby and Duke of Leeds, 1632–1712* (Glasgow, 1944–51, 3 vols).

For the agricultural crisis of the 1660s and beyond, see Joan Thirsk, *The Agricultural History of England and Wales*, vol V (1640–1750), part ii (Cambridge, 1984–5), and M. G. Davies, 'Country gentry and falling rents in the 1660s and 1670s', *Midland History*, IV (1977–8), 86–96. For economic change more generally, see C. G. A. Clay, *Economic Expansion and Social Change: England 1500–1700* (Cambridge, 2 vols, 1984); see D. C. Coleman, *Sir John Banks, Baronet and Businessman* (Oxford, 1963) and C. G. A. Clay, *Public Finance and Private Wealth* (Oxford, 1978) for an impression of the relationship between government and business in the period.

R. Macgillivray, *Restoration Historians and the English Civil War* (The Hague, 1974), gives an account of royalist and parliamentarian views of the past: Andrew Sharp, 'Edward Waterhouse's view of social change in seventeenth-century England', *Past and Present*, no. 62 (1970), 27–46 describes one man's view of the present. See also Jonathan Scott, *Algernon Sidney and the English Republic, 1623–77* (Cambridge, 1987) for the historical perspectives of the regime's radical opponents. For the political theory of royalism, see J. W. Daly, *Sir Robert Filmer and English Political Thought* (Toronto, 1979), and M. Goldie, 'John Locke and Restoration anglicanism', *Political Studies*, XXXI (1983), 61–95.

John Miller gives an overview of the relationship between Restoration governments and parliaments in 'Charles II and his parliaments', *Transactions of the Royal Historical Society*, 5th series, XXXII (1982); Derek Hirst has replied in 'The conciliatoriness of the Cavalier Commons reconsidered', *Parliamentary History*, V.ii (1987). Generally, on Charles II's ambitions and his opportunities, see John Miller, 'The potential for "absolutism" in later Stuart England', *History*, LXIX (1984), and 'The Later Stuart Monarchy', in *The Restored Monarchy*, ed. J. R. Jones (London, 1979).

Perhaps the most important work on Restoration government published in the last twenty years is C. D. Chandaman's *The English Public Revenue, 1660–1688* (Oxford, 1975). Henry Roseveare, *The Treasury, 1660–1870: the foundations of control* (London, 1973), and S. B. Baxter, *The Development of the Treasury, 1660–1702* (London, 1957) describe the treasury reforms instituted during the period: but there is still no adequate account of the problems of the government's credit system, which is central to its inability to sustain major expenditure for long. P. G. M. Dickson, *The Financial Revolution in England* (London, 1967), describes the changes of the 1690s which would modernise the system. Other facets of government administrative reform are discussed by Howard Tomlinson, *Guns and Government: the ordnance office under the later Stuarts* (London, 1979), and by J. C. Sainty, 'A reform in the tenure of offices during the reign of Charles II', *Bulletin of the Institute of Historical Research*, XLI (1967), 150–71.

The legislative progress of the Restoration settlement, at least in the Cavalier Parliament, is described in Paul Seaward, *The Cavalier Parliament and the Reconstruction of the Old Regime, 1661–1667* (Cambridge, 1989). Denis Witcombe, *Charles II and the Cavalier House of Commons, 1663–1674* (Manchester, 1966) is a largely narrative account of politics. Andrew Swatland, 'The Role of Privy Councillors in the House of Lords, 1660–81', in Clyve Jones (ed.), *A Pillar of the Constitution: the House of Lords in British Politics, 1603–1784* (London, 1989) is an account of parliamentary management, for which, see also Browning, *Danby*, J. R. Jones, 'Parties and Parliament' in his *The Restored Monarchy*, and Clayton Roberts, *Schemes and Undertakings: a study of English politics in the seventeenth century* (Columbus, Ohio, 1985). Richard Davis, 'The "Presbyterian" opposition and the emergence of party in the House of Lords in the reign of Charles II', in *Party and Party Management in Parliament, 1660–1784* (Leicester, 1984) argues (a little too far) for the religious origins of political opposition. See also D. R. Lacey, *Dissent and Parliamentary Politics in England, 1661–89* (New Brunswick, 1969). The theory of the constitution is discussed in C. C. Weston and J. R. Greenberg, *Subjects and Sovereigns: the grand controversy over legal sovereignty in Stuart England* (Cambridge, 1981): for a corrective (though for an earlier period) see J. P. Sommerville *Politics and Ideology in England, 1603–1640* (London, 1986).

For local government, see Anthony Fletcher, *Reform in the Provinces: the government of Stuart England* (London, 1986); C. G. F. Forster, 'Government in Provincial England under the later Stuarts', *Transactions of the Royal Historical Society*, 5th series, XXXIII (1983); S. K. Roberts, *Recovery and Restoration in an English County: Devon local administration, 1646–1670* (Exeter, 1985). A. M. Coleby, *Central Government and the Localities: Hampshire 1649–1689* (Cambridge, 1987) argues that Restoration local government had the strength and self-confidence that its Interregnum counterpart lacked: P. J. Norrey, 'The Restoration regime in action: the relationship between central and local government in Dorset, Somerset, and Wiltshire, 1660–1678', *Historical Journal*, XXXII (1988), 789–812, gives a different view. See also M. A. Mullett, 'Conflict, politics and local elections in Lancaster, 1660–1688, *Northern History*, XIX (1983), 61–86. J. H. Sacret, 'The Restoration government and the municipal corporations', *English Historical Review*, XLV (1930), 232–59 is criticised by John Miller, 'The Crown and the borough charters in the reign of Charles II', *English Historical Review*, C (1985), 53–84. For the gentry in local politics and government, see James Rosenheim, 'County

Government and Elite Withdrawal in Norfolk, 1660–1720', in *The First Modern Society: Essays in English History in honour of Lawrence Stone*, ed. A. L. Beier, David Cannadine and James Rosenheim (Cambridge, 1989); Norma Landau, *The Justices of the Peace, 1679–1760* (Berkeley, 1984); and Philip Jenkins, *The Making of a Ruling Class: the Glamorgan gentry, 1640–1790* (Cambridge, 1983). See M. A. Kishlansky, *Parliamentary Selection: social and political choice in early modern England* (Cambridge, 1986). Urban politics, and especially popular politics, are described by Tim Harris, *London Crowds in the Reign of Charles II: propaganda and politics from the Restoration to the Exclusion crisis* (Cambridge, 1987), and see also his 'The Bawdy House riots of 1668', *Historical Journal*, XXIX (1986), 537–56. Charles II's army is described by John Childs, *The Army of Charles II* (London, 1976), and see his companion volume, *The Army, James II, and the Glorious Revolution* (Manchester, 1980).

The conflict of old presbyterians and royalists during the Restoration has received little attention, despite its importance for the future development of the whig and tory parties. See P. H. Hardacre, *The Royalists during the Puritan Revolution* (The Hague, 1956); and for the land issue, see J. Thirsk, 'The sales of Royalist land during the Interregnum', *Economic History Review*, 2nd series, V (1952/3), 188–207; H. J. Habakkuk, 'Landowners and the English Civil War', ibid., 2nd series, XVIII (1965), 130–51; P. G. Holiday, 'Land Sales and Repurchases in Yorkshire after the Civil Wars, 1650–1670', in *Northern History*, V (1970), 67–92; J. Broad, 'Gentry Finances and the Civil War: the case of the Buckinghamshire Verneys', *Economic History Review*, 2nd series, XXXII (1979), 183–200; and P. Roebuck, *Yorkshire Baronets 1640–1760: Families, Estates and Fortunes* (Oxford, 1980). See also Seaward, *Cavalier Parliament*, ch. 8. For Danby's stimulation of anglican royalist feeling, see R. A. Beddard, 'Wren's mausoleum for Charles I and the cult of the Royal Martyr', *Architectural History*, XXVII (1984), 36–49.

For the political importance of religion, see M. G. Finlayson, *Historians, Puritanism, and the English Revolution: the religious factor in English politics before and after the Interregnum* (Toronto, 1983), and Tim Harris, 'Introduction', in *The Politics of Religion in Restoration England*, ed. Tim Harris, Mark Goldie and Paul Seaward (Oxford, 1990). The best standard account of the Restoration Church is the brief one by Robert Beddard, 'The Restoration Church', in Jones's *The Restored Monarchy*; when published John Spurr's forthcoming *The Restoration Church of England, 1646–89* will be the best there is. I. M. Green, *The Re-establishment of the Church of England, 1660–1663* (Oxford, 1978), concentrates on the physical restoration of the Church, although he also discusses the politics of its re-establishment, as does R. Clark, 'Why was the re-establishment of the Church of England in 1662 possible? Derbyshire: a provincial perspective', *Midland History*, VIII (1983); Robert Bosher, *The Making of the Restoration*

Settlement: the influence of the Laudians, 1649–1662 (Westminster, 1951) uses rather suspect categories, but is still the best basic account of the political process of re-establishment that exists. See also G. R. Abernathy, 'The English presybterians and the Stuart Restoration, 1648–1663', *Transactions of the American Philosophical Society*, new series LV, part 2 (1955), and Seaward, *The Cavalier Parliament* for the religious legislation of 1661–5. Religious politics in parliament are also dealt with in D. R. Lacey, *Dissent and Parliamentary Politics* and by John Spurr, 'The Church of England, comprehension, and the 1689 Toleration Act', *English Historical Review*, CIV (1989), 927–46. For the discussions on toleration and comprehension, see R. Thomas, 'Comprehension and indulgence', in *From Uniformity to Unity, 1662–1962*, ed. O. Chadwick and G. F. Nuttall (London, 1962) and see also Anne Whiteman, 'The restoration of the Church of England', in the same volume. For the arguments over toleration, see Richard Ashcraft, *Revolutionary Politics and Locke's 'Two Treatises of Government'* (Princeton, 1986), particularly ch. 2; Mark Goldie, 'The Huguenot experience and the problem of toleration in Restoration England', in *The Huguenots and Ireland: anatomy of an emigration*, ed. C. E. J. Caldicott, H. Gough and J-P. Pittion (Dublin, 1987), pp. 175–203; and the introduction to *John Locke: two tracts on government*, ed. P. Abrams (Cambridge, 1967).

The local studies mentioned above contain a good deal about the religious politics of the localities, but see also Anthony Fletcher, 'The enforcement of the Conventicle Acts, 1664–1679', in *Persecution and Toleration*, Studies in Church History, XXI (Oxford, 1984), pp. 233–46; J. J. Hurwich, 'A "Fanatick town": the political influence of dissenters in Coventry, 1660–1720', *Midland History*, IV (1977), 15–48; and the essays in *The Politics of Religion in Restoration England*, ed. Tim Harris, Mark Goldie and Paul Seaward (Oxford, 1990).

G. R. Cragg, *Puritanism in the Period of the Great Persecution* (Cambridge, 1957) is still an important study of dissent: but for an introduction to the sects see, now, J. F. Macgregor and B. Reay, *Radical Religion in the English Revolution* (Oxford, 1984); and N. H. Keeble, *The Literary Culture of Nonconformity* (Leicester, 1986). For the quakers, see B. Reay, *The Quakers and the English Revolution* (London, 1985), 'The authorities and early Restoration quakerism', *Journal of Ecclesiastical History*, XXXIV (1983), 69–84, and 'The quakers, 1659, and the Restoration of the monarchy', *History*, LXIII (1978), 193–213. For the baptists, see Christopher Hill, *A Turbulent, Seditious and Factious People: John Bunyan and his Church* (Oxford, 1988). See, for presbyterianism, W. M. Lamont, *Richard Baxter and the Millenium: protestant imperialism and the English revolution* (London, 1979). The introduction by Anne Whiteman to *The Compton Census of 1676*, British Academy Records of Social and Economic History, new series, vol. X (Oxford, 1986), is illuminating on the extent and geographical spread of the problem of dissent, as well as for dissenters' behaviour.

For the Church's economic problems, see J. H. Pruett, *The Parish Clergy under the Stuarts: the Leicestershire experience* (Urbana, Illinois, 1978); one of the best studies, however, is an unpublished thesis: E. A. O. Whiteman, 'The episcopate of Dr Seth Ward, bishop of Exeter and Salisbury' (University of Oxford, D.Phil., 1951). For its religious attitudes, see G. R. Cragg, *From Puritanism to the Age of Reason: a study of changes in religious thought within the Church of England, 1660 to 1700* (Cambridge, 1950), John Spurr, '"Latitudinarianism" and the Restoration Church', *Historical Journal*, XXXI (1988), 61–82 (cf. M C. Jacob, *The Newtonians and the English Revolution* (London, 1976) and J. Marshall, 'The ecclesiology of the latitude men, 1660–1689: Stillingfleet, Tillotson and "Hobbism"', *Journal of Ecclesiastical History*, XXXVI (1985)).

Anti-popery and the catholic issue in English politics are well described by John Miller, *Popery and Politics in England, 1660–1688* (Cambridge, 1973). See also K. H. D. Haley, '"No popery" in the reign of Charles II', in J. S. Bromley and E. H. Kossman (eds), *Britain and the Netherlands*, V (The Hague, 1975), 102–19.

Keith Feiling, *British Foreign Policy, 1660–1672* (London, 1930), is a useful introduction to its subject. R. A. Stradling's unpublished Ph.D. thesis, 'Anglo-Spanish relations, 1660–1668' (University of Wales, 1968) is the only recent treatment of a large and otherwise neglected area in Charles II's foreign policy. Relations with the Netherlands are treated in Charles Wilson, *Profit and Power: a study of England and the Dutch wars* (Cambridge, 1957); for a more recent account see Jonathan Israel, *Dutch Primacy in World Trade, 1585–1740* (Oxford, 1989), and 'Competing cousins: Anglo-Dutch rivalry', in *History Today*, XXXVIII (July, 1988), 17–22. The dynastic side of Anglo-Dutch relations is described in Pieter Geyl, *Orange and Stuart, 1641–72* (London, 1969). The making of the war of 1665–7 in English domestic politics is described in Paul Seaward, 'The House of Commons committee of trade and the origins of the second Anglo-Dutch war, 1664', *Historical Journal*, XXX (1987), 437–52. For the diplomacy which led to the Triple Alliance and the war of 1672–4, see K. H. D. Haley, *An English Diplomat in the Low Countries: Sir William Temple and John De Witt* (Oxford, 1986); for the more shadowy negotiations which led to the secret Treaty of Dover, see Ronald Hutton, 'The making of the secret Treaty of Dover, 1668–1670', *Historical Journal*, XXIX (1986), 297–318. See S. B. Baxter, *William III* (London, 1966) and K. H. D. Haley, *William III and the English Opposition 1672–1674*, for the war of 1672.

For popular perceptions of England's standing abroad, see Peter Furtado, 'National pride in seventeenth-century England', in *Patriotism: the making and unmaking of British national identity*, ed. R. Samuel (3 vols, London, 1989), I, 45–56. For a republican view, and for a general discussion of 'interest' theory, see Jonathan Scott, *Algernon Sidney and the English Republic, 1623–1677* (Cambridge, 1988). For the navy, see Bernard Capp, *Cromwell's Navy: the fleet and the English revolution, 1648–1660* (Oxford, 1989), to which J. D. Davies's thesis, 'The seagoing personnel of the Navy, 1660–1689' (Oxford D.Phil., 1986), will, when it is published, be a useful sequel; see his 'Pepys and the Admiralty Commission of 1679–84', *Historical Research*, LXV (1989), 34–53. F. Fox, *Great Ships: the battlefield of Charles II* (Greenwich, 1980) provides some useful appendices. For the navy's activities in the Mediterranean, see S. Hornstein, *The Deployment of the English Navy in Peacetime, 1674–1688* (Leiden: Rijksuniversiteit te Leiden, 1985).

There is a large literature on England's foreign trade in the later seventeenth century. It is most accessibly described by C. G. A. Clay, *Economic Expansion and Social Change: England, 1500–1700* (2 vols, Cambridge, 1984), II, 'Industry, trade and government'. But see also K. N. Chaudhuri, 'Treasure and trade balances: the East India Company's export trade, 1660–1720', *Economic History Review*, 2nd series, XXI (1968), 480–502, and *The English East India Company* (London, 1965); K. G. Davies, *The Royal African Company* (London, 1957); G. F. Zook, 'The Company of Royal Adventurers trading into Africa', *Journal of Negro History*, IV (1919); R. Davis, *English Overseas Trade, 1500–1700* (London, 1973), and 'English foreign trade, 1660–1700', *Economic History Review*, 2nd series, VII (1954); and, for the political debate over the 'balance of trade', see M. Priestley, 'Anglo-French trade and the "unfavourable balance" controversy, 1660–1685', *Economic History Review*, 2nd series, IV (1951). For the organisation of English trade in the Mediterranean, see S. P. Anderson, *An English Consul in Turkey: Paul Rycaut at Smyrna, 1667–1678* (Oxford, 1989).

For the colonies, see S. S. Webb, *The Governors-General: the English army and the definition of the Empire* (Williamsburg, 1979), '"Brave men and servants to his royal highness": the household of James Stuart in the evolution of English imperialism', *Perspectives in American History*, VIII (1974), 55–60, and *1676: the end of American independence* (Cambridge, Mass., 1985). See also J. M. Sosin, *English American and the Restoration Monarchy of Charles II: transatlantic politics, commerce and kinship* (University of Nebraska, Lincoln), 1980. For the government's oversight of trade and the colonies, see C. M. Andrews, *British Committees, Commissions, and Councils of Trade and Plantations, 1622–1675* (Johns Hopkins University studies in Historical and Political Science, XXVI, Baltimore, 1908).

The political crises of the 1680s have received a good deal more attention than the rest of the reign. J. P. Kenyon, *The Popish Plot* (Harmondsworth, 1974) is a straightforward account of the details of the plot itself. The politics of the period (and beyond it) may be followed in Haley's *The First Earl of Shaftesbury*, and in J. P. Kenyon's biography of *Robert Spencer, Earl of Sunderland* (London, 1958). J. R. Jones, *The First Whigs: the politics of the exclusion crisis, 1678–83*

(Oxford, 1961), is an account of the origins of whiggism that is now a little outdated, although there is as yet no single account to replace it. The meanings of the plot are examined by Jonathan Scott, in 'England's troubles: exhuming the popish plot', in *The Politics of Religion in Seventeenth-century England*, ed. Harris, Goldie and Seaward, and 'Radicalism and Restoration: the shape of the Stuart experience', *Historical Journal*, XXXI (1988), 453–67. Scott's *Algernon Sidney and the Restoration Crisis 1677–83*, shortly to be published, will provide a challenging re-interpretation of the meaning of the crisis. The arguments of whigs and tories are discussed in O. W. Furley, 'The whig exclusionists: pamphlet literature in the exclusion campaign', *Cambridge Historical Journal*, XIII (1957), 19–36; R. Ashcraft, *Revolutionary Politics and Locke's 'Two Treatises of Government'*, and J. G. A. Pocock, *The Ancient Constitution and the Feudal Law: a study of English historical thought in the seventeenth century* (reissue, Cambridge, 1987), ch. 8. On tory argument, see James Daly, *Sir Robert Filmer and English Political Thought*, G. J. Schochet, *Patriarchalism in Political Thought* (Oxford, 1975), and Mark Goldie, 'John Locke and anglican royalism'.

D. F. Allen discusses two aspects of the crisis in 'The political role of the London trained bands in the exclusion crisis, 1678–81', *English Historical Review*, LXXXVI (1972), 287–303, and 'Political clubs in Restoration London', *Historical Journal* XIX (1976), 561–80. London in the crisis is also discussed by Harris, *London Crowds in the Reign of Charles II*, and by Gary De Krey, 'London radicals and revolutionary politics, 1675–83', in *The Politics of Religion in Seventeenth-century England*, ed. Harris, Goldie and Seaward, and 'The London whigs and the Exclusion crisis, reconsidered', in *The First Modern Society*, ed. Beier, Cannadine and Rosenheim, pp. 457–82. For the relationship of nonconformity and whiggism see, besides the works quoted above concerning religion, H. Horwitz, 'Protestant reconciliation in the exclusion crisis', *Journal of Ecclesiastical History*, XV (1964), 201–17.

The reaction from whiggism is described by R. A. Beddard, 'The retreat on toryism: Lionel Ducket, member for Calne, and the politics of conservatism', *Wiltshire Archaeological Magazine*, LXXII/LXXIII (1980), 75–106. For the struggle for power in the City, see J. Levin, *The Charter Controversy in the City of London* (London, 1969), and for elsewhere, see R. G. Pickavance's 1976 Oxford D.Phil thesis, 'The English boroughs and the king's government: a study of the tory reaction, 1681–1685', unfortunately not published. It is criticised by John Miller in 'The Crown and the borough charters in the reign of Charles II'. See R. A. Beddard, 'The commission for ecclesiastical promotions, 1681–84: an instrument of tory reaction', *Historical Journal*, X (1967), 11–40, for the Yorkist trend in the Church after 1681. J. R. Western, *Monarchy and Revolution: the English state in the 1680s* (London, 1972), shows how the monarchy was strengthened in the mid-1680s, although he also provides a narrative account of James II's reign and the revolution.

Bibliography

W. A. Speck, *Reluctant Revolutionaries: Englishmen and the revolution of 1688* (Oxford, 1988) is a clear account of the reign and the revolution and is a useful guide to current historiographical debates. J. R. Jones, *The Revolution of 1688 in England* (London, 1972) is still helpful. Monmouth's rebellion is treated by Peter Earle, *Monmouth's Rebels* (London, 1977), and R. Clifton, *The Last Popular Rebellion: the Western rising of 1685* (London, 1984). The expansion in James's army is described by John Childs, *The Army, James II and the Glorious Revolution*. P. E. Murrell gives an account of the local effects of the campaign to pack parliament, in 'Bury St Edmunds and the campaign to pack parliament, 1687–8', *Bulletin of the Institute of Historical Research*, LIV (1981), 188–206. The painful divorce of Church and king is considered in G. V. Bennett, 'The seven bishops: a reconsideration', in *Religious Motivation*, Studies in Church History, XV (1978), 267–87, and 'Loyalist Oxford and the revolution', in *The History of the University of Oxford*, ed. L. S. Sutherland and L. G. Mitchell (Oxford, 1986). R. A. Beddard, 'Vincent Alsop and the emancipation of Restoration dissent', *Journal of Ecclesiastical History*, XXIV (1973), 161–84, discusses the implications for the dissenters. The revolution itself, and its meaning, are examined by W. A. Speck, 'The Orangist conspiracy against James II', *Historical Journal*, XXX (1987), 453–62, D. Hosford, *Nottingham, Nobles and the North* (Hamden, Conn., 1976), and J. P. Kenyon, *The Nobility in the Revolution of 1688* (Hull, 1963). G. H. Jones, 'The Irish fright of 1688', *Bulletin of the Institute of Historical Research*, LV (1982), 423–35 describes the fear that gripped England during the Revolution. And see R. A. Beddard, *A Kingdom Without a King: the journal of the provisional government in the Revolution of 1688* (Oxford, 1988) for a useful and readable account of the Interregnum, and the essential removal of James.

Few recent attempts have been made to set the Restoration firmly into context: it remains in a sort of historical limbo, different to the pre-1640 world, but not quite the eighteenth century. J. C. D. Clark, *Revolution and Rebellion: state and society in England in the seventeenth and eighteenth centuries* (Cambridge, 1986), attempts vigorously to change the context. J. H. Plumb, *The Growth of Political Stability in England, 1675–1725* (London, 1967), has set an agenda for the discussion of later seventeenth-century politics, but historians have done little since to try to refine and debate his points, at least for this period. The views of John Miller on government policy ('The later Stuart monarchy', in *The Restored Monarchy*, ed. J. R. Jones), on the potential for 'absolutism' ('The potential for "absolutism" in later Stuart England'), and on parliament ('Charles II and his parliaments'), Jonathan Scott's argument concerning the 'Restoration crisis', Mark Kishlansky's argument for the 'politicization' of county life, and the developing interest in religion as the cause of political conflict (e.g. Tim Harris, 'Introduction' in *The Politics of Religion in Restoration England*, ed. Harris, Goldie, Seaward) may prove fertile areas of debate.

167

INDEX